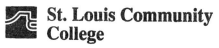

AT-RISK "PARENT AND FAMILY" SCHOOL INVOLVEMENT

Strategies for Low Income Families and African-American Families of Unmotivated and Underachieving Students

ABOUT THE AUTHOR

Gary Reglin has taught mathematics and managed a successful dropout retention program in Florida public schools. The program was featured on television, in the February 1990 edition of *The Technological Horizons in Education Journal,* and visited by the Governor. He has published thirty journal articles and book chapters, and presented at seventeen refereed national and state conferences. His most recent book is *Motivating Low-Achieving Students: A Special Focus on Unmotivated and Underachieving African-American Students.* The author teaches "Analysis of Teaching" and "Instructional Design and Evaluation" to preservice teachers. He teaches two graduate courses to inservice educators, "At-Risk Strategies" and "Effective Parental Involvement and Parental Education Strategies for Educators." He conducts workshops for all grade levels.

AT-RISK "PARENT AND FAMILY" SCHOOL INVOLVEMENT

Strategies for Low Income Families and African-American Families of Unmotivated and Underachieving Students

By

GARY L. REGLIN, ED.D.

Assistant Professor
Department of Curriculum and Instruction
University of North Carolina at Charlotte
Charlotte, North Carolina

CHARLES C THOMAS • PUBLISHER
Springfield • Illinois • U.S.A.

Published and Distributed Throughout the World by

CHARLES C THOMAS • PUBLISHER
2600 South First Street
Springfield, Illinois 62794-9265

© *1993 by* CHARLES C THOMAS • PUBLISHER

ISBN 0-398-05877-6

Library of Congress Catalog Card Number: 93-19838

With THOMAS BOOKS *careful attention is given to all details of manufacturing
and design. It is the Publisher's desire to present books that are satisfactory as to
their physical qualities and artistic possibilities and appropriate for their particular
use.* THOMAS BOOKS *will be true to those laws of quality that assure a good
name and good will.*

Printed in the United States of America
SC-R-3

Library of Congress Cataloging-in-Publication Data

Reglin, Gary L.
    At risk "parent and family" school involvement : strategies for
low income families and African-American families of unmotivated and
underachieving students / by Gary L. Reglin.
        p.   cm.
    Includes bibliographical references (p.   ) and index.
    ISBN 0-398-05877-6
    1. Home and school—United States.   2. Education—United States—
Parent participation.   3. Socially handicapped children—Education—
United States.   4. Afro-American children—Education.   I. Title.
LC225.3.R44   1993
649′.68—dc20   93-19838
                                                                          CIP

With love and thankfulness,
this book is dedicated to my children,
Kedra Reglin and Sebastian Reglin.

PREFACE

The book was written for preservice teachers, inservice teachers, Chapter I teachers, parent involvement coordinators, counselors, school administrators, parents, and staff development coordinators at the elementary, middle grades, and the secondary levels. The purpose of this book is to serve as a guide and to provide the aforementioned persons with a set of innovative strategies effective in getting low socio-economic status (SES) and African-American families meaningfully involved in the educational process of their children, thus motivating the children to achieve and behave better in the public schools.

Most of the suggestions, activities, strategies, and models have been tried and proven to be successful. Two recent situations will be shared with the readers that reinforce the need for this text. In February 1993, I gave a presentation at the 4th Annual Conference on Youth At-Risk in Savannah, Georgia. I shared many of my ideas in this text with the seventy-eight educators who were present at the session in a presentation titled "Involving Low Income and Minority Parents of Underachieving Students: Some Effective Strategies." During and after the conference, the educators commented that the information was badly needed in the public schools because it was practical and adaptable for immediate school and classroom usage. Additionally, many public schools are beginning to make family involvement a number one priority. This is manifested in a recent initiative by John Murphy, Superintendent of the Charlotte-Mecklenburg School System, one of the largest in the state of North Carolina. Also in 1993, Superintendent Murphy introduced Proposed Policy #1230. At the top of the policy in bold letters are the statements, "THE PROPOSED POLICY #1230," PARENT/FAMILY INVOLVE-MENT, AS SHOWN BELOW, IS UNDER CONSIDERATION BY THE BOARD OF EDUCATION. IT IS TO BE POSTED FEBRU-ARY 12-25, 1993 IN ALL SCHOOLS AND DEPARTMENTS OF THE SCHOOL SYSTEM. SUGGESTIONS FOR MODIFICATIONS SHOULD BE SENT TO THE SUPERINTENDENT'S OFFICE."

This text is especially valuable for preservice and new teachers. It should be a part of all universities' teacher preparation programs. The text can be used as a supplementary text for any graduate or undergraduate course on "Dropout Prevention." It is also suitable as a "stand alone" text for any course on parental involvement strategies. I have used much of the information in the book in two courses that I teach. The courses are "At-Risk Strategies" and "Effective Parental Involvement and Parent Education Strategies for Educators."

Many preservice teachers and new teachers have a difficult time working with low income and African-American families whose students are unmotivated and underachieving. Many of these families feel intimidated by the teachers, and teachers feel threatened by the families. These feelings usually result from a lack of understanding and communication rather than because of lack of concern about the child's education. I have seen many preservice teachers quit during student teaching as a result of negative experiences during field activities with these families. Numerous new teachers have requested transfers from schools with large numbers of these families and students as quickly as possible to the more affluent suburbs. This text will provide practical and easy to implement strategies in each chapter to increase the successes and decrease the mental anguish that preservice educators and teachers are encountering with many unmotivated and underachieving students from low income and African-American families. The author encourages readers of the book to copy activities and strategies and share them to facilitate parent/significant family member—teacher cooperative efforts.

When the author was organizing the manuscript for this book, five logical chapters emerged. Chapter One brings to the reader's attention the need to innovate in the public schools. Tradition is a valuable and comforting source of stability. However, sometimes tradition no longer adequately serves the educational needs of all students in the public schools. When the demands made on us as educators change, then the way that we prepare for them must change. Innovation means looking beyond what is and envisioning what could be. Innovation when working with many low SES students and African-American students means not limiting school involvement efforts to the traditional biological parents but seeking and encouraging other "significant" family members to maintain high visibility in the public school education of their children. A "parent and family focus" for this text is defined as effective strategies targeted at low SES and African-American "significant" family members to encourage them to become highly visible in meaningful educational activities of their children. It views interactions between parents and educators as a two-way street. Two queries are made in this process. They are, "How can parents and family members help the school and how can the school help meet the needs of parents and family members?"

Chapter One asserts that public school administrators must reconfigure school records to reflect information that teachers will require to assist them in locating "the right, significant family member for the right job in the public schools." It is important that a good **match** is made so that both the public schools and the families can benefit. Teachers must also have sufficient information to reveal hobbies/interests of family members, degree of contact with non-custodial parents, and other related items crucial to effective decision making and avenues of participation in school activities. The information in the computer databases and the schools' cumulative folders on the children must be somewhat reflective of the questions that are presented by the "Parent and Family Profile Model" developed by the author.

The author concludes Chapter One with several additional reasons why many low income and African-American students are not motivated to achieve. The reasons revolve around the author's experiences with educators and students at one of the highly rated public schools in the state. Based on standardized test scores and report cards, all groups of students were achieving at this school except the African-American students, particularly African-American males. At this school, there were few racial problems and most of the underachieving African-American students presented almost no discipline problems. Attendance was good. Yet, the minimum discipline problems and regular attendance did not translate into good grades or good test scores for the African-American students. These students were very difficult to "reach" even when the teachers consistently employed the best of teaching and nurturing techniques. It is this author's contention that all students can achieve and the strategies presented in subsequent chapters of this text will motivate these students to achieve.

Chapter Two discusses noninvolvement issues related to single parent families and African-American families. Many unmotivated and under-achieving low SES and African-American students are in single parent families. Schools need special strategies to address the single parent situation. Family structures are becoming increasingly diversified. Single-parent families, remarried families, "his, hers, and ours" families, and parent-friend families are increasingly changing the norm of family living, especially for the poor. Poor parents are nearly twice as likely to break up as those who aren't poor, the government reported in January 1993 in its first study of how financial hard times cause families to dissolve. When a marriage breaks up, three times out of four a mother and her children who were above the poverty line tumble below it. The resulting stress causes many children to sit silently with blank stares on their faces in the classrooms. These students' stress-filled minds will cause them to "tune academics out." Others channel the stress related energy into disruptive classroom behavior. Some will create classroom discipline problems solely for the purpose of engaging the teacher in classroom confrontations that will be an outlet for their negative, stress-driven behavior.

Principals and teachers can address the needs of children of single parent families through school policies and practices. This text provides an "Awareness, Reflection, and Action Model" to effectively assist educators in this endeavor. This is a training model for educators to use as part of staff development and is specifically designed to encourage involvement of low income, single-parent families in the school process. This involvement will enhance the academic motivation and achievement of their children. Five activities are in the model: Attending School Functions, Addressing Financial Concerns, Insensitivities, Positive Adult Role Models, and Non-Custodial Parent Involvement. In the latter part of the chapter, some general principles and "tips" are delineated that schools can follow to enhance African-American families' involvement in the educational process. The secrets underlying the principles and "tips" are: know who the family members are, assess their needs and talents by employing reliable and valid measures, provide personalized services at the schools with an "invitational" approach and personalized services that will adequately address their needs, invite them to come into the school and use their talents, be careful not to coerce them into making long term commitments to school projects, and show genuine appreciation for their efforts. Educators will also benefit from employing the Minority Involvement Model (MIM).

Chapter Three indicates that there are large numbers of teachers who have had negative experiences with endeavoring to get low SES and African-American "significant" family members involved in the school process. These negative experiences oftentimes resulted in "bad attitudes." The teachers perceived themselves as professional "baby-sitters" and disciplinarians instead of educators. Ten reasons are provided by the author that "feed" some teachers' negative attitudes toward family involvement. Examples of the reasons: (1) The classroom is perceived as the teacher's responsibility and he/she is unwilling to "let go," and (2) Teachers believe these families are often engaged in multiple pathologies such as drug abuse and illiteracy (Burland, 1984). The author contends that when teachers have good attitudes and good experiences concerning family involvement, all persons in the learning milieu of the children will benefit tremendously. When teachers help low income and African-American family members to help their children, these family members can be as effective with their children as those parents with more education and leisure time. Sixteen helpful suggestions for teachers are shared that will transform "bad attitudes" into "good attitudes." Examples are "catching family members being good," employing good interpersonal skills, training the family members for the tasks, and establishing an informational card system.

Chapter Three contends that all low SES and African-American parents and family members are talented. These talents can be used as a basis for enhancing school involvement. Initially, the teacher must ascertain what the talents are by surveying parents or through phone interviews. The text provides some helpful open ended questions that can be used in the interview and survey process. The questions are in the "Parent/Family Interview or Survey Model." When the teacher has collected data from the surveys and has discovered the resources available through the parents and family members, he/she must then consider ways in which these skills, interests, etc., can be used in the school or in the classroom. For example, a parent may have an interest in music or basketball. The parent with the interest in music may be referred to the assistant principal to assist with any musical event that will occur at the school in the near future. The family member with an interest in basketball may be assigned as a counselor or mentor for underachieving students who are on the basketball team or who are involved in the YMCA youth basketball league. The rationale is that students are more responsive to adults with whom they perceive a common bond or connection.

After data collection employing the "Parent/Family Interview or Survey Model," the next step is for the teacher to extend an "invitation" to assist with school activities using the "Parent/Family Opportunities Survey." To ensure a good return rate on the survey forms, teachers need to reward students by having popcorn, pizza, balloons, or cookies and ice cream parties for the class with the best return rate. Once the parent or family member has consented to participate in the school activities, it is vital that they are trained or briefed prior to being assigned to the task. The two models/surveys can be beneficial in another important way. They will make the classroom "come alive" and provide many "real life" experiences that a substantial number of low income and African-American students don't have. Most of these students have very limited access to enrichment experiences. School budgets and time constraints usually allow few field trips.

Chapter Four indicates that effective efforts can be made by school administrators to decrease families' alienation. This should be high on the agendas of all principals because family involvement is found to directly affect student achievement. Schools cannot operate in a vacuum. They need the support of all families. Principals must lead the crusade to bring parents/families of low income and African-American students into the school, not just as passive participants or volunteers, but as full partners between the parent/families and the professional (Sandfort, 1987). Seventeen suggestions to assist principals are delineated. I am aware that school administrators will be unable to implement all of the suggestions offered. However, school administrators should be capable of implementing some of the suggestions. Implementing only a few should yield significant dividends that will be reflected in enhanced student motivation and achievement. Examples of the suggestions are: employing a variety of school involvement strategies, having a parent/student switch day, hiring parents as teacher aides and substitute teachers, holding activities at the site of major employers, having a family appreciation night, establishing a multicultural climate, and ensuring that the initial thrust at involvement is social.

A paramount reason why families will not become involved in school activities is that the families have many needs that are not being satisfied. Principals can effectively address this issue by realizing that parents have diverse needs, many of which can be addressed to some extent through viewing the needs from the perspective of Maslow's *Hierarchy of Needs.* Numerous examples of satisfying needs are presented for each level of the hierarchy. For instance, survival needs can be somewhat satisfied through employing parents as clerical and maintenance workers, hosting General Educational Development (GED) courses at night, and providing word processing classes and computer classes. Security needs can be somewhat satisfied through safety presentations and self-defense classes by police officers for parents during evening hours. Three additional strategies for principals that are effective are briefly discussed. Principals can establish and maintain Parent Centers. The purpose of parent centers is to get parents to feel more positive about the school and more welcome in the school (Stevens, 1992). The Centers should offer some morning, afternoon, and evening hours to accommodate working and non-working parents. Home Visiting and a Home Visitor Program can be established. Home visiting is an effective means of providing parents/ families and teachers a time for exploring their common concerns, sharing information on child development and learning, and laying a foundation for having a positive relationship (Young Children, 1990).

The purpose of the Home Visitor Program is to have parents or family members who are recruited, interviewed, and paid to go into the housing projects or other low income neighborhoods to recruit additional family members into the schools, or to disseminate information and materials concerning school activities. These coordinators will be a liaison between the teachers, counselors, social workers, and the families living in low income neighborhoods. The coordinators should be parents/family members who are actively involved in the community such as deacons in churches, officers in local civic groups, and other leaders in churches or community organizations. They should be well respected and should have lived in the community for a substantial number of years.

Chapter Five briefly discusses two additional topics of concern. The first topic is "Incidental Learning Through Role Models." Low SES and many African-American students learn much from family members through incidental learning that is carried into the classroom. Incidental learning is a social learning term denoting that children learn by watching an influential adult role model's behavior and the consequences of the behavior. The model may be verbalizing one message but his or her behavior may be sending a different and a more negative message to the children. If there is a discrepancy between parents' preaching and parents' practice, children will tend to do as the parents do, not as they say. Five suggestions are provided to assist teachers in advising parents/family members on how to use modeling and incidental learning to support teachers' academic efforts in the classroom. The second topic is "Asian-Americans' Parental Expectations." Asian-Americans comprise approximately two percent of the national population, but they earn 2.6 percent of all bachelor degrees and 3.4 percent of all doctoral degrees awarded each year. Information is shared with educators from a study exploring the cultural factors of Asian-American high school students that will guide low SES and African-American families to better take charge of the after school activities of their children.

The author hopes that the readers will find *At-Risk "Parent and Family" School Involvement: Strategies for Low Income Families and African-American Families of Unmotivated and Underachieving Students* to be as useful and as practical as it was intended to be. I have attempted to be as brief and straightforward as is feasible and to use terms which can easily be understood by parents/family members, preservice educators, and veteran educators. My wish is that teachers, low SES families, and African-American families can become educational partners and can work together meaningfully, enjoyably, and productively so that the educational experiences of all children will be more meaningful, enjoyable, and effective. Strategies and activities delineated in this text will cause a significant increase in parent/family involvement in the school life of the child. This augmented and positive involvement will engender a more motivated teacher, a more motivated student, and higher achievement scores for all students in the classroom.

ACKNOWLEDGMENTS

This book, like almost all others, could not have been written without invaluable support from many people. The author wishes to express his gratitude and thanks to all those who gave words of encouragement and assistance as I gathered this information. Special acknowledgement goes to Ms. Glynda Manning, Chapter I Parent Involvement Coordinator from Charlotte-Mecklenburg County. Glynda provided many ideas and much information in the preparation of this text. I would also like to acknowledge the teachers, counselors, dropout prevention coordinators, and school administrators in my two graduate courses, "At-Risk Strategies" and "Effective Parental Involvement and Parent Education Strategies for Educators." They offered me a chance to present my ideas and made a number of crucial suggestions about fundamental aspects of the work. Kim Ryder, a teacher at Randolph Middle School and a graduate student at the University of North Carolina at Charlotte, pursuing a Masters Degree in English, devoted many hours in proof reading the manuscript. Kim provided many suggestions that are incorporated in the text. I wish to express my gratitude and thanks to four significant persons that have given me considerable encouragement and strength throughout my adult life, without which none of my accomplishments would be possible. These important people are my Father, Willie Reglin, Sr.; daughter Kedra; son Sebastian; and my loving sister Rena Mae Matthews.

CONTENTS

AT-RISK "PARENT AND FAMILY" SCHOOL INVOLVEMENT
Strategies for Low Income Families and African-American Families of Unmotivated and Underachieving Students

Chapter One

INTRODUCTION

"PARENT AND FAMILY FOCUS" FOR THE 1990S

The survival of all our children (poor, rich, African-American, Hispanic, American Indian, Asian-American, and White) depends on how well parents and educators unite in support of each other. Children make up 40 percent of the population and 100 percent of our future. Abraham Lincoln said: "A child is a person who is going to carry on what you have started. He is going to sit where you are sitting, and, when you are gone, attend to those things that you think are important. The fate of humanity is in his hands." As parents and educators, we must prepare all children to have a successful future. All children wish to and are able to succeed. We can assure success in the public schools with all children if educators and parents acquire the courage and vision to experiment with better ways of teaching, parenting, and molding effective parent-school partnerships.

We must innovate in the public schools. Tradition is a valuable and comforting source of stability. But, sometimes, tradition no longer adequately serves to meet the educational needs of all students in the public schools. When the demands made on us as educators change, then the way that we prepare for them must change. Innovation means looking beyond what is and envisioning what could be. Innovation means not limiting school involvement efforts to the traditional biological parents but seeking and encouraging other significant family members to maintain high visibility in the public school education of children.

A significant family member could be any family member with strong ties to the child. Examples may be grandmothers, stepparents, foster parents, older brothers and sisters, or uncles and aunts. Grandmothers and/or grandfathers may be the basic caregiver for several reasons, including: (1) the natural parent has abandoned the children, (2) the child is illegitimate and the parent has turned over responsibility for childrearing to the grandparent, and (3) the parent may not be physically able or mentally competent to provide adequate care for the child. There are a rapidly increasing number of grandparents becoming the basic caregivers for low socioeconomic status (SES) and African-American families. A significant family member may also be a nonfamily member who has a strong bond with the child. This situation often reflects the term, friend, which is in vogue among single parents today. Many single parents live with a boyfriend or girlfriend who assist in the upbringing of the child. The presence of this adult cannot be overlooked or ignored but must be included in any effort toward parent and family involvement. Innovation means a parent/family focus as opposed to primarily focusing on promoting school involvement of biological parents for the 90's.

A parent/family focus for this text is defined as effective strategies targeted at low socioeconomic status and African-American significant family members to get them to become highly visible in meaningful educational activities of their children. It views interactions between parents and educators as a two-way street. Two queries are made in this process: they are, "How can parents/family members help the school and how can the school help meet the needs of parents/family members?" This comprehensive definition recognizes parents/family members as having talents and skills which can be used for their own welfare and well-being as well as the welfare of their children and school. At the same time the definition recognizes that families have many needs which can be met through school involvement including: physical, mental, social, and emotional needs.

The definition includes advocacy: low income and minority parents sitting on councils and committees, participating in the decisions and operations of schools. It includes grandmothers serving as substitute teachers and teachers' assistants. It means aunts and fosterparents accompanying classes on outings, being parent center coordinators, or assisting teachers in a variety of ways, either as volunteers or for wages. It means children's thirty-one year old single sisters or sixty-two year old grandfathers initiating learning activities at home to improve the children's performance in school, such as: reading to them, helping them with homework, playing educational games, discussing current events, and so on (Ascher, 1988). Throughout this text, a term which will be used frequently is parent/family involvement. Parent/family involvement for this text is defined as any significant or influential member of the child's family becoming actively involved in the educational process or maintaining high visibility in the educational process of the child.

Having the children's own parents, or people like their parents, in the school will make a big difference to the academic program (Brandt, 1986). Children will hurry out of their classrooms after classes to show their papers to their significant family members, and they won't act in troublesome ways because they want to maintain the respect of both the family members and the teachers. Because families and teachers will be in agreement, they will be working together as an academic team. There should be no way for children to play one adult authority figure against another. The results will be a tremendous improvement in students' academic motivation, academic achievement, social behavior, and attendance. Also, there will be improvements in family members' positive behaviors. When significant family members witness children succeeding in school, feeling good about the successes, and perceiving the successes are in part due to their contributions, the family members will put forth more focus on their own good behaviors and less focus on the negative behaviors.

There are a rapidly growing number of unmotivated and underachieving low SES and African-American students whose achievement could be enhanced greatly if family members demonstrated concern in the students' academic efforts and maintained high visibility in key school academic and social activities. Superintendents and principals should design schools' computer databases and students' school folders with pertinent data on all significant family members. Therefore, if the teacher is unsuccessful at getting the biological parents involved, data on other family members can be readily accessed. Presently, few public schools have their records organized to rapidly and accurately obtain this type of data. Creating databases with this information would be a worthwhile and a feasible project. The information can be acquired from diverse sources, including: biological parents, students, census records, government agencies, community records, and church records. Presently, information is not available at numerous schools due to the tradition of focusing on the concept of biological parent involvement instead of parent/family involvement. This tradition must change if we are to ensure the public school success of many unmotivated and underachieving low SES and African-American students.

In the numerous workshops that I conducted as part of inservice training for public school teachers at the elementary, middle grades, and high school levels, many of them expressed intense frustrations because of an inability to get the biological parents of low SES and African-

American students involved in the education of their children. The teachers were adamant in their beliefs that the noninvolvement engendered profound student motivation problems. Teachers stated that many of these students are unmotivated, underachieving, and creating significant behavioral problems. Also, they expressed that a substantial number of the students were not creating discipline problems, but they were not motivated to complete academic assignments, participate in class activities, or ask questions. They simply came to school unprepared, sat in class, and became silent with an indifferent attitude for the entire class period.

Another recent experience of mine in 1992 deeply affected and reinforced in me the need to write this text. Mark, a history teacher in a rural high school in North Carolina, told me that many of his students did not take advantage of the school's "reteach" program. This is a program wherein students who failed a major test would be allowed to retake the test if they attended the voluntary "reteach." In the "reteach" class, designated teachers were available before and after class to teach or review the testing areas with the students. After completion of the "reteach," the students would be allowed to take a makeup test to improve the test grade.

Mark informed me of a typical incident where twelve of his twenty-nine students failed a major exam. He encouraged all of them to attend the "reteach," so they would be eligible to take his makeup exam. He emphasized to them that most students who attended the reteach in the past were successful in passing the makeup exams. Mark pointed out that passing the exam was critical to passing the course. Of the twelve students, only one attended the reteach.

Mark was a superior educator. I observed his class on several occasions. He used many of the latest teaching techniques, was very caring, enjoyed his profession, and enjoyed the students. He had been teaching for thirteen years and possessed a Masters Degree in History. Mark was offered several lucrative teaching positions at nearby community colleges. All of them were refused because he perceived his "calling" was to teach high school youths. I was impressed with his enthusiasm and determination to go "above and beyond the call of duty" and to ensure that all students succeeded. Desperate for help, an invitation was extended to me to give a motivational talk to the students.

All students were from low income families. Of the twelve students, ten were males and two were females. Nine students were African-

Americans and three were White. The twelve were described by teachers at the school as good students relative to behavior. This meant that they created few discipline problems and were "nice" and respectful to adults. They would sit, listen, and acknowledge the teacher, yet devote little effort and motivation to academics. These students were underachieving and unmotivated, even though they had superior and caring teachers. I interviewed all of the students' teachers and they expressed similar concerns relative to subpar academic motivation. This situation was not unique to this school or to the high school environment but is replicated at other rural schools, urban schools, middle schools, and elementary schools throughout the nation.

After my motivational talk to the students, I conversed with them on an individual basis. My intentions were to ascertain the reasons for their lackadaisical attitude towards education and to come up with effective recommendations to enhance their school motivation. I discovered a common element in these students which greatly disturbed me: no adult in the family took the time out or made the time to get actively involved in their education. No significant member from the family had been to any of the school's activities, except an occasional basketball or football game. No family member tutored, worked as a substitute teacher, worked as a teachers' assistant, served as a chaperone on field trips, or answered the phone in the central office. No one assisted with school functions on a voluntary or paid basis. I informed Mark that a prime source of the students' subpar motivation was due to lack of family involvement and family members' high visibility in school activities.

Mark informed me that he consistently attempted to contact the biological parents and that many of them lived in single parent homes with the mother being the head of the household. He revealed that the parent or parents portrayed an indifferent attitude concerning school involvement. Many were too busy working several jobs endeavoring to pay for the necessities of life. Others said, "The child is your problem while he is at school. You are his teacher and you should be able to do your job and motivate him. Isn't that what you went to college for?" After numerous phone calls to no avail, Mark became frustrated due to the indifferent attitudes parents had about their children's education. Instead of exploiting his creative juices and exploring the parent/family alternative, his perception was that he was fighting insurmountable odds and would not be successful. He finally gave up trying to get the biological parents involved. I asked him if there was a profile or any records of other key persons in the students' lives, such as members of the extended family that may have the time, willingness or capability to get involved in the school. Mark replied that his school records were not organized to yield this type of information.

The environment at Mark's school was not conducive to encouraging involvement from the extended family. This was shocking in that many low SES and African-American students live with, or were greatly influenced by, great-grandparents, grandparents, uncles, aunts, brothers, sisters, or cousins. If they don't live in the houses of these family members the majority of the time, students spend a great deal of time at their houses. Many of Mark's students lived with single parents who were too busy struggling with survival needs to become actively involved with school. The education of the children was not at the top of the priority list. Some of the students lived with parents who were intimidated by the bureaucracy and bigness of the school. They had experienced many failures in school which engendered a reluctance to get involved.

Based on my extensive research, I have discovered that some family members can always be located who want to get involved in the school. I will provide a recent example of a teacher gaining much mileage from pursuing my concept of parent/family involvement. In one of my 1993 workshops for teachers, a "Teacher of the Year" shared with me an incident concerning one of her students. The sixth grader's name was Craig. Craig mother's Susan was thirty-four years of age and a single parent. She was receiving little child support from Craig's deadbeat father and had to work two jobs to take care of the family's basic survival needs, which included apartment rent, food, and clothing. Susan worked full time from 6 A.M. to 2 P.M. (Monday through Friday) and part-time from 3 P.M. to 6:30 P.M. (Monday through Friday) at the second job. Susan did not have enough time or energy to get involved and assist in Craig's school activities. She also had little time, energy, or patience to assist Craig with his homework during the week. Therefore, his academics suffered. He began failing, even though he had the potential to be an excellent student. According to his teacher, the child was not a behavior problem. He had simply lost all motivation to do any type of academic work.

After numerous futile attempts at battling with Susan to quit her part-time job, lower her living standards, and devote more time to assisting Craig's academic efforts; the "Teacher of the Year" decided to identify and solicit the help of another significant member of the family.

She talked extensively with Craig and Susan and discovered that Craig had a great-grandmother who was sixty-seven years of age, energetic, willing, and had lots of time to come to school on a frequent basis to assist in some of the school functions. The great-grandmother and Craig had a very loving and close relationship. She would take care of him many days after school, while Susan was working. Also, Craig visited her frequently on the weekends. Yet, no educator had previously extended an invitation to her to assist in the school. The "Teacher of the Year" extended the invitation and the great-grandmother accepted it. However, the teacher was very careful to make the great-grandmother feel wanted, capable, and sure that her efforts would increase the probability of Craig having success in school.

The great-grandmother was willing to do anything within her ability to assist in the academic development of her great-grandson. She had limitations: she did not have a car and only had a ninth grade education. She did not feel comfortable answering questions about Craig's home-work but she agreed to make sure that he devoted the necessary time to complete the homework and that he explained it to her. The teacher and administrators assisted in coordinating and providing transportation to the school by contacting local churches and community members. Together they created a list of names of people who would be elated in sharing the responsibility of providing transportation to the school and to school related events held in the community. They would take turns transporting her.

The teachers at the school fell in love with the great-grandmother because of her warm, outgoing, and friendly personality. They discovered that she had natural counseling skills and a bubbly personality that attracted the kids to her. Because of this talent, she was asked to talk with many shy students. The end result was that the great-grandmother began devoting much of her time in not only helping Craig but benefitting the school in many other ways. This was a two-way partnership that every-one cherished. Because of her presence in the school, Craig's school motivation and achievement improved. He looked forward to seeing his great-grandmother in the school. He felt someone in his family really cared about his education and future success. His education and future success became important, and Craig became more "turned on to school." The teacher benefitted from the partnership in that the teacher had more time to devote to nurturing and teaching the other students.

Craig's mother, Susan, mysteriously started appearing at the school on some days and at many evening school activities. She was overheard several times, boasting to teachers and parents about Craig's good grades and the positive comments on his report card. Susan began reassessing her priorities. Communications with the teacher became more frequent, and inquiries were made about joining the local Parent Teachers Association and the parent advisory council. She enrolled in a community college to pursue a ten month paralegal course. She felt that working as a paralegal would give her more time to be with Craig and to become a more active part of his academic efforts. The author is aware that not all family involvement efforts by educators will be this successful; but my experiences clearly reveal that most efforts will have a significant positive impact on the motivation and achievement of poor students and African-American students who are underachieving.

It is my assertion that the following statement should be written into the philosophy of all public schools: "All students can achieve success in the public schools with high visibility and use of the talents of significant family members." This is certainly a powerful statement in that only eight percent of a child's time is spent in school while 92 percent of his/her time is spent outside of the school with peers and significant family members. If family members are effectively involved in the education of their children by teaching their kids and guiding them through learning activities outside of school, this eight percent will be greatly increased. This is because the home will become an extension of the school and family members will be functioning as teachers or teachers' helpers. Family support, family encouragement, and family visibility in the school are critical ingredients in low SES and African-American students' success in school.

In a study released in 1990 by the National Assessment of Educational Progress, researchers found that school attendance, outside reading, homework, and television watching affected the math performance of students of low income parents. These are all activities that influential family members can positively impact. It is vital that educators support my concept of parent/family involvement during the kindergarten and early elementary school years of low SES and African-American students. The support should be in the form of adequate funding, staffing, and recruiting of family members as paid helpers or volunteer workers. This is the time when families are more concerned with factors impacting the learning of their kids. If educators focus on the early formative years, this will engender adolescents to be responsible and successful students in middle school and high school. Families have a proclivity to become more involved in the school activities during middle school and high school years when their children are making good grades, and the parents are the recipients of myriad positive messages from the teachers.

Senator Bill Bradley's statements indicate the importance of "catching kids early." "Who are the kids who will be entering the kindergarten next year?" he asked. "One in four of them lives in poverty, one in five is going to be a teen parent, one in two comes from a family where both parents work and where the parents cannot afford adequate child care. This is the generation who will be the first high school graduates in the 21st century" (Bradley, 1988). It is the author of this text's assertion that by focusing on parent/family involvement during the early school years and by employing my techniques expounded in subsequent chapters, high school graduates in the 21st Century will be assets instead of liabilities. This focus will eliminate kids' serious misbehaviors that are presently occuring in my county and throughout the nation. Students are showing disrespect for education; they are fighting, poisoning, and shooting teachers. Schools, parents, and families are supporting this disrespect by not working as partners.

Involvement of families can bring stability to the academic lives of students and counteract the instabilities low SES and African-American students encounter in school. These instabilities are further manifested in the differential treatment of the students by teachers, which again, reinforces failure. Family members can serve as an ongoing support system for children, and, thus, have a consistent influence on their education and development (Prosise, 1990). Many low SES children have different teachers year after year. The different teachers usually have different expectations for behaviors and academics. Many of the teachers have low expectations for achievement and conduct for these students. Others expose them to a wide variety of teaching strategies in order to find one that works. However, these differences and the experimenting can confuse low income students and further hinder academic achievement and motivation. If family members are actively involved in the educational activities of the students, they can provide some stability and a consistency of expectations and behaviors which a school cannot offer.

Current research supports the need for public schools to steer away from the traditional notion of biological parent involvement. Davies (1987) argued that the new definition of parent involvement must evolve to a broader definition to portray reality. Davies contended that family is a more encompassing term. The new definition, family involvement, should also include not only those parents who readily respond to teacher and school initiatives but also the families that schools consider "hard to reach." The latter group (which in some schools include a majority of low income, Hispanic, American Indian, and African-American families) includes those who lack the energy, time, self-confidence, or English language proficiency to take part in traditional parent involvement activities, as well as those who are fearful of schools because of past experiences or cultural norms. According to Davies, in most schools, activities that fit the old definition of parent involvement engage only a relatively small number of parents, who provide leadership and service and who are aware of the advantages of such involvement to themselves and their own children. And, of course, it is the upper and middle class children who benefit the most.

As stated before, public school administrators must reconfigure school records to reflect information that teachers will require to assist them in locating "the right family member for the job." Teachers must also have sufficient information to reveal any hobbies and interests of family members, the degree of contact with noncustodial parents, and other related items crucial to effective decision making and avenues of participation in school activities. The information in the computer databases and the school's cumulative folder on the children must be somewhat reflective of the questions in my Parent and Family Profile Model. The model which is presented below is intended only as a guide. Teachers may add questions, delete questions, or revise questions as necessary. The final model should reflect concerns of the teachers and of the school.

Parent and Family Profile Model

Name of Student _____ Birthdate _____

Directions: Counselors or the school social workers should be the coordinating point for data collection. At a faculty meeting, they should give each teacher a "Parent and Family Profile Model" form to complete. Teachers should phone the biological parent or guardian and request information on the twelve questions. If the information from the biological parent or guardian is insufficient to complete the profile, communicate with other family members, churches, community agencies, or the applicable government agencies. All forms should be returned to the designated coordinator who will check to ensure each item has been completed. Secretaries should assume primary responsibility for inputting the information in the school's computer database or the children's school folders.

Purpose: To collect information on the extended family that can be used to assist teachers in decision making and in encouraging a member of a student's family to be actively involved in promoting the educational success of the student. However, this information will be used only after extensive efforts to obtain involvement from one or both of the biological parents have been tried, and the efforts have been futile through no fault of the public school educator. This data should not be used to replace existing student data but should supplement existing information to reflect the rapidly changing traditional nuclear family, particularly for low SES and African-American families.

Rationale: The traditional non-nuclear family has drastically changed due to myriad and diverse reasons. Parents of many students are difficult to get actively involved in the educational efforts of their children. The reasons may be beyond the control of the parents. This profile is not an attempt to place blame on parents. However, research shows vividly that students are more motivated when someone from the family is actively and visibly involved in their academic activities. There are a rapidly escalating number of low SES students who are unmotivated and under-achieving due in a large part to subpar or zero parental/family involvement. The twelve item profile was designed to effectively address this issue.

Profile Items: The information on the card should be updated annually. Elements for inclusion on the card might be:

1. Please list the full names of the following family members:

Mother _____ , Father _____ ,

Stepparent _____ , Friend _____ ,

Aunts _____ , Uncles _____ ,

Grandparents _____ , Great-Grandparents _____ ,

Brothers _____ , Sisters _____ ,

(Indicate Brothers and Sisters whose ages exceed 20 years).

* A "friend" is defined as a single mother's or single father's boyfriend or girlfriend who visits or stays with the single parent on a frequent basis and with whom the single parent enjoys an intimate relationship. This may include gay and lesbian relationships.

2. Please list the full addresses of the following family members:

Mother _____ ,   Father _____ ,

Stepparent _____ ,   Friend _____ ,

Aunts _____ ,   Uncles _____ ,

Grandparents _____ ,   Great-Grandparents _____ ,

Brothers _____ ,   Sisters _____ ,

(Indicate Brothers and Sisters whose ages exceed 20 years).

3. Please list the occupations of the following family members:

Mother _____ ,   Father _____ ,

Stepparent _____ ,   Friend _____ ,

Aunts _____ ,   Uncles _____ ,

Grandparents _____ ,   Great-Grandparents _____ ,

Brothers _____ ,   Sisters _____ ,

(Indicate Brothers and Sisters whose ages exceed 20 years).

4. Please list any hobbies and interests of the following family members:

Mother _____ ,   Father _____ ,

Stepparent _____ ,   Friend _____ ,

Aunts _____ ,   Uncles _____ ,

Grandparents _____ ,   Great-Grandparents _____ ,

Brothers _____ ,   Sisters _____ ,

(Indicate Brothers and Sisters whose ages exceed 20 years).

5. Provide phone numbers and "best-times-to-reach" information on the family members:

Mother _____ ,   Father _____ ,

Stepparent _____ ,   Friend _____ ,

Aunts _____ ,   Uncles _____ ,

Grandparents _____ ,   Great-Grandparents _____ ,

Brothers _____ , Sisters _____ ,

(Indicate Brothers and Sisters whose ages exceed 20 years).

　6. Does the child live in a single parent household?

Yes _____ , No _____ ,

Custodial Parent

_____

Non-custodial Parent

_____

　7. Please indicate the dates of separation and/or divorce, and of remarriage:

Date of Separation

_____

Date of Divorce

_____

Date of Remarriage

_____

　8. Please approximate the number of weeks of contact the child had with the noncustodial parent during the last six months:

Weeks of Contact

_____

　9. Please write a brief statement on any changes in school performance since the divorce/separation/remarriage:

Changes in School Performance

_____

_____

_____

10. Please provide names of school personnel with knowledge of the family situation:

Custodians _____ , Secretaries _____

Cafeteria Workers _____

Teachers _____ , Administrators _____

Bus Drivers _____

Others _____

11. Please write a brief statement regarding important changes in the family (visitation, births, employment, etc.): _____

_____

_____

12. Please write any additional comments you feel may be critical to obtaining involvement of family members: _____

_____

_____

It is essential that innovations are put into place that are effective in addressing the large numbers of unmotivated students. In numerous schools, I have heard principals complain about the lack of motivation that students and parents have toward academic endeavors. When I query them to ascertain exactly which students and parents are in this predicament, the responses are always students and parents who are low SES, African-American, Hispanic, and American Indian. For instance, at an urban school in Charlotte, NC, one principal invited me to her school to share strategies on motivating students. The principal informed me in a conference that she was concerned about the African-American students, principally the African-American male students. Many of the African-American students were from low income families.

At this school, the standardized test scores of the African-American male students were far lower than all other groups (Morris, 1992). The school had about 40 percent White students and 60 percent African-American students. There were few racial problems and most of the underachieving African-American students presented few discipline problems. Attendance was good. However, the minimum discipline problems and regular attendance did not translate into good grades or good test scores. These students were very difficult to reach even when the teachers consistently employed the best of teaching and nurturing techniques. There is no one reason for this situation. However, my research, interviews with educators, and experiences reveal several paramount reasons.

(1) The low income and minority student population are increasing at a phenomenal rate. By 1995, one-third of American public school

students in sixteen states and Washington, D.C., will be Hispanic or non-white, according to a two-year study by the College Board and the Western Interstate Commission for Higher Education. According to the study, all racial and ethnic groups will see an increase in student enrollment, but Whites will lose ground as a percentage of the total student population. Most of the minority students will be from low income families.

(2) The shortage of minority teachers, particularly African-American teachers is increasing at a phenomenal rate. For example, the last ten public middle schools and elementary schools in which I gave workshops averaged three African-American teachers out of 30 certified teachers. The African-American student population at these schools was between 40 percent and 60 percent of the total student population.

(3) Class size in the average public school classroom still "hovers" around thirty students per class which is too large for students of the 90's because of the tremendous social problems these students bring into the classroom.

(4) The majority of the public school teachers are White, middle-class females, who are having a difficult time teaching and disciplining poor and African-American students. Nationally, 95 percent of the teachers hired in 1992 were White. Many are not familiar with the cultures and habits of the students, particularly the African-American male students. This unfamiliarity engenders fear, a "hands-off" and "teaching from a distance" approach to teaching. There are major initiatives underway to recruit more minority teachers in the teaching profession. More businesses are giving teaching scholarships to minorities, South Carolina has established an effective Teacher Cadet Program, North Carolina has a successful Teaching Fellows Program, and many school districts are establishing Speaker Bureaus. Speaker Bureaus are a pool of enthusiastic teachers who go into the community and talk about the positive aspects of teaching. However, it may be many years before these initiatives engender significant numbers of African-American teachers.

(5) The majority of the African-American teachers are middle-class females who are having a difficult time teaching and disciplining low SES African-American students. They attended predominantly White private schools and White Universities. During their adolescent years, these teachers lived in the mostly White, middle income suburbs. Their patience with poor children is very short. Their patience with poor African-American male youths is even shorter. Many are not familiar

with the culture and habits of low income students, particularly low income, African-American male students. This unfamiliarity engenders fear, and a "hands-off" and "teaching from a distance" approach to teaching.

(6) Educators have not been successful in getting many parents of low SES and African-American students involved in the education of their children. This is primarily because of the use of traditional and non-aggressive methods. A parent/family member being highly involved in school activities positively correlates with greater student achievement and motivation. Low parent/family involvement engenders student apathy, more student misbehaviors, frustrated teachers, and students who may eventually be a substantial liability on society.

SUMMARY

Parent/family involvement benefits teachers. Low SES families and African-American families who participate in involvement programs are more positive about the teacher's abilities. In other words, teachers who work at family involvement are considered better teachers than those who remain more isolated from the families of the children they teach. Parents have needs that teachers must try to meet. After years of being told that they don't know "the right way to raise their children," parents need to have their confidence restored. Teachers will have to convince parents to believe in themselves and once again regard themselves as significant educators of their children.

Teachers must become as involved in teaching family members their important role in their children's education as they are in teaching the children themselves the rudiments of education. Though teachers must struggle with this dual responsibility, the pay-off of well adjusted and educated children is worth the effort. Achievement scores will soar upwards, and safety and discipline in the classroom will no longer be a top issue. As educators, we know that without a healthy self-esteem a child cannot learn. Because they spend more time with their children than teachers do, family members must give their child a positive image of themselves.

All research clearly suggests that parent/family involvement in the education of the child is important in terms of the child's self-esteem, academic motivation, school achievement, and later success in life. In summarizing a number of longitudinal studies, Lazar and Darlington

(Consortium for Longitudinal Studies, 1981) noted that factors directly related to family involvement (such as home visits by the teacher that focus on both the parent and the child, and the development of specific program goals designed to involve parents in the education process) led to a program's effectiveness, as measured by children's achievement during a certain period of time. Another finding consistently relates student achievement to parental attitudes, both toward themselves and toward their child's education.

The basic idea that seems to emerge from many of these studies is that the more parents feel in control of their lives, the more likely their child is to do well (Hess, 1980). In terms of family attitudes about education, again the theme seems to be that the more interested and involved significant family members are in the child's education, the better the child does. For example, children do better when a significant family member takes the initiative in finding out what the child is doing in school, when they are able to relate easily to teachers, when they show an interest in what the child brings home from the school, when they provide activities at home to extend the child's school experience, and when they present the school experience in a positive light to the child. The more involved low SES and African-American families are, the more they want to continue and expand this involvement (Smith, 1980).

ACTIVITIES FOR THE READERS

1. Discuss the definition of parent/family involvement with another teacher, a school official, a counselor, a low SES parent, and a business person. What are the similarities in their definitions? What are the differences?

2. How much inservice training have you had concerning parent involvement? How much exposure have you had concerning effective techniques relative to parent/family involvement in your training as a preservice teacher? Was this sufficient? Explain.

3. Observe a rural high school class over a period of one week. Determine the students who participate in discussions and volunteer to answer questions. Write their names on your paper. Determine the students who do not participate in discussions and volunteer to answer questions. Write their names on your paper. Ask the teacher which students are on the free or reduced lunch list. Ask the teacher which students' parents or family members are actively involved in the school

or have high visibility in school functions. Construct a table with the following items:

Name of Student, Participating in Class or Nonparticipating, High/Middle Income or Low Income, High Parent/Family Involvement or Low Parent/Family Involvement.

Synthesize your information, look for trends, draw inferences from your data, and provide recommendations based on your findings. This information should be assembled in the form of a report. Present it to your class.

4. Discuss all possible reasons why a student may not want to go to a reteach, even though it is clear to the student that attendance at the reteach will probably lead to passing the makeup test and subsequently passing the course. How will you relate this information to the parent or significant family member. What advice would you give them? Write six specific points that you would say to the student in a one-on-one student-teacher conference. How would you respond to a principal who would say that it is your responsibility to motivate the child to attend the reteach.

5. Discuss at least six major reasons why many low SES families and African-American families appear not to want to get involved in the educational process of their child. Why would some high and middle income parents be reluctant to get involved? Compare and contrast the two. Abraham Maslow in his "Hierarchy of Needs" contends that families' lower needs must be fulfilled to some extent before they will go to their higher needs. Explain how you can use this premise to promote school involvement of low SES families. Can or should the school be in the business of satisfying their needs? Why or Why not?

6. What is meant by teachers having differential expectations for high and low achieving students in the classroom? How can usually low expectations in academic achievement and behavior for low income and minority students be a self-fulling prophecy for these students. Do some teachers have differential expectations for low income and high/middle income families relative to school involvement? Why or why not? What would be the effect on student achievement?

7. Go to a school and ask the teacher for assistance in completing the "Parent and Family Profile Model" on each student in the class. Organize your data and present a report to the teacher or your university class. Ensure that the report is as detailed as feasible. Are you surprised

by your findings? Why or Why not? Be sure to include in your report how you plan to use this information to promote high visibility of parents/families in the school.

8. Interview five low income or African-American family members with high visibility in the educational activities of their children. You should go to the assistant principal or counselors for the names of the family members. Discuss with them what they enjoy most about being involved. Get suggestions from them to enhance the involvement of "hard to get" parents/families.

9. Invite church ministers, public service agencies, or leaders of community programs to your classroom. What specific services do they provide to meet the immediate needs of parents? What services do they provide to assist students? What partnerships do they have with the schools?

10. In what ways has the family changed in the past twenty years? Do you approve of the changes? Why? Why not? How has the role of the children in the family changed? What new roles do the children have?

Chapter Two

MAKING SENSE OF NONINVOLVEMENT

SINGLE PARENTS' NONINVOLVEMENT

Many unmotivated, underachieving low SES and African-American students are from single parent families. That is not to say that all children in single parent families have low motivation and low achievement. There are many of these children who are well adjusted and very successful public school students. However, as will be clearly presented later on in this chapter, there are a substantial number of these kids who are failing. Schools need special strategies to address the single parent situation. Schools desperately need special strategies to promote productive participation of the noncustodial parent, as well as the custodial parent, in the academic life of the child. As indicated by Duncan (1992), the traditional nuclear family, in which the biological children and their parents live in a single family dwelling, is no longer the dominant family scene in America.

Family structures are becoming increasingly diversified. Single-parent families, remarried families, "his, hers, and ours" families, and parent-friend families are increasingly changing the norm of family living, especially for the poor. Divorce and separations among low SES parents compound the problems that their children bring into the classroom. Children face an immediate psychological problem when their environment undergoes the changes that a loss of a biological parent brings. In a remarried family, where one parent with custody of children marries a second, or possibly third time, additional complexities emerge.

Poor parents are nearly twice as likely to break up as those who aren't poor, the government reported in January 1993 in its first study of how financial hard times cause families to dissolve. One out of seven married couples below the poverty line splits up, compared with one out of thirteen couples with higher incomes, the Census Bureau reported in a study that tracked families for two years in the 1980s. In addition, when a marriage breaks up, three times out of four a mother and her children who were above the poverty line tumble below it. In 1991, a married couple with one child was considered poor if the family earned less than $10,963 a year; with two children, less than $13,812; and with three children, $16,254. "This report is a striking reminder of the ways in which strong family values have to include strong economic foundations for families," said Clifford Johnson, family support director for the Children's Defense Fund. "We've known intuitively for a long time that poverty and other economic problems create a lot of stress for parents and children." Educators must contend with this stress which manifests itself in the form of a poor mindset by the parent and child. This, in turn, precludes or reduces school involvement by the parents and prevents parents from putting the education of their children first on their priority list. The effects of this stress hinders good classroom participation and performance by the students (Reglin & Amen, 1992).

The stress is heavy on the students' mind while class is in progress. Therefore, students' minds will not become receptive to classroom teaching. Some will sit silently with blank stares on their faces. Others channel the stress related energy into disruptive classroom behavior. Some will create classroom discipline problems solely for the purpose of engaging the teacher in classroom confrontations that will be an outlet for their negative, stress-driven behavior. According to Clifford Johnson, a marital split not only results in stress for parents and children but additionally sends poor families further into poverty, as the father's departure slashes income. For the children, it may mean poor health, learning disabilities and eventual unemployment. There were 103,800 families in the Census Bureau study; each was tracked for one of several two-year periods from 1983 through 1988. Marital splits included separations and divorces.

If the present trends continue, 60 percent or more of today's children will spend some time in single-parent homes before their eighteenth birthdays. Most of these children will spend as many as six years in homes with only one parent (Sweet & Bumpass, 1988). These children have needs that affect school programs. Their academic achievement may lag as they have trouble concentrating, worrying about their family situations, or suffering from poor self-concept. Children who have trouble adjusting to single-parent homes also may behave inappropriately in school (Wanat, 1991). As the number of students from single-parent families increases, schools must consider how they can provide the special support these students need, even if the students don't ask for assistance.

In many instances, divorce has removed the father from the home and left the care of the children to a working mother or a mother living on welfare payments. Economic concerns drive the working mother to work long hours outside the home. Thirty percent of school age children will see their families dissolve by divorce. These figures are even higher for African-Americans, American Indians, and Hispanics (Carlson, 1990). Studies show that children from single parent families are more likely to show behavioral problems; some of these problems include: absenteeism, tardiness, truancy, inefficient study habits at home, and disruptive classroom behavior. Based on recently released data from the U.S. Census Bureau, African-American children living with just one parent increased from 31.8 percent in 1970 to 45.8 percent in 1980 and 57.5 percent as of March 1991. Of the 5.8 million African-American children living with one parent, the vast majority, 5.5 million, live with the mother, the report said. Sar Levitan, director of Social Policy Studies at George Washington University, said the figures from the U.S. Census Bureau reflect the "deterioration of the American family structure." The trend is serious because one-parent families more often live in poverty. "The child's chances of living in poverty are six times as high as they would be in a two-parent family," he said.

Adults other than a child's parents are taking on significant child-rearing roles. While the extended family's involvement in childrearing is not new among African-Americans, the scope of that involvement is growing. Parents who thought that their child-rearing days were over are increasingly raising their grandchildren. In the last twenty years, the percentage of African-American children being raised by a grandparent has risen from 3.2 percent to 12.5 percent (or one in eight) (Edwards & Young, 1992). Households with children under eighteen years of age now commonly include foster parents, extended families, children living with other relatives, adoptive parents, or reconstituted and blended families. Many of the potential dropouts that the author of this text has worked with were the products of single parent families with the mother being the head of the household. Many others were from a dual parent families with the mother and father working several jobs; so they had little time to tend to the cognitive and affective needs of their children (Reglin, 1993).

Togerson (1990) found that "little had been done and little was being planned on a district basis to program inservice dealing with single-parent children." Barney and Koford (1987) concurred, noting that schools have continued to react slowly and with a "lack of sensitivity to the very apparent societal changes going on around us." Principals and teachers can address the needs of children of single parent families through school policies and practices. The critical steps in this process are:

1) **Teacher Awareness.** Teacher awareness is important because many teachers are not aware of the unique problems associated with single parent families that impede their children's achievement in the classroom.

2) **Teacher Reflection.** Teacher reflection is vital because teachers are very busy during a normal school day and have little time to reflect on the behaviors of single parent children. They also are unable to set aside sufficient time to reflect on solutions to the negative behaviors of these students.

3) **Teachers' Collaborative Input into Decision Making.** Teachers will be reluctant to support any solutions unless the teachers are an important part of the decision making process. Teachers work with these children and parents/family members closer than other school personnel. Therefore, teachers input should be highly valued.

4) **Implementation and Monitoring of an Action Plan.** Any action plan involving single parents and their children will significantly impact the classroom. Teachers are the most important persons in the success or failure of the action plan.

Principals must implement staff development activities to encourage school personnel to become aware of and reflect on the paramount concerns of single parent families. Many low SES and African-American single parent families will not become actively involved in the education process until their unique concerns are understood and adequately addressed through an effective action plan. Below is my "Awareness, Reflection, and Action Model." It is a training model designed to encourage involvement of single parent families. The activities in the model are based on the aforementioned critical four steps.

Awareness, Reflection, and Action Model

Activity #1: Attending School Functions

What the Inservice Training Leader Should Do:

1. Group the faculty and staff into groups of five or six. The inservice training leader should try to group the faculty as close as possible based on similar disciplines. For example, math teachers should be grouped

together and English teachers should be in the same group. Groups should be allowed to leave the current meeting room and work in any classroom in the school. Groups are more effective when they can work in a comfortable, familiar, and an informal setting.

2. Designate one person as the group facilitator and one person as the group recorder. The task of the facilitator is to encourage each group member to voice an opinion, and to ensure the group communication does not digress from the assigned topic. The inservice training leader should endeavor to assign counselors or social workers as facilitators, where feasible. The functions of the recorder are to record all information germane to the topic, inform the group when five minutes are remaining in the allotted time for the task, inform the group when all time has elapsed, and summarize the recorded information at the faculty meeting when requested by the inservice training coordinator.

3. Tell the group that this is a thirty minute awareness, reflective, and action activity designed to enhance the school involvement of single parents. Display the rationale for the group activity on the overhead and read it to the faculty. Display the group activity questions on the overhead. Tell the group to find a comfortable classroom to work in and to report back to the central location in thirty minutes.

Rationale for Activity #1:

Involvement of single parents in the school is critical to the school motivation and the school achievement of the child. Innovative strategies are required to improve the school involvement of single parents, particularly single parents who are in a low SES. Single parents have difficulty meeting with teachers and attending school functions during the day. Single parents usually work two or three jobs to take care of food, housing, and clothing needs. Survival is typically at the top of their priority list. Therefore, pursuing the money from the two or three jobs will take precedence over school involvement. The group task is to share ideas, engender realistic and innovative strategies to improve school involvement, and provide a five to ten minute report to the faculty.

Procedures for Activity #1:

Prepare group responses for each of the questions. What are the 10 major school and classroom activities you feel that parents should assist with or should attend? Which of the above would be especially difficult for single parents based on the information in the rationale? Explain why. How can these activities be modified to promote better participation by single parents? For example, would it be feasible to have the activities at night, on the weekends, at a local church, at the YMCA, etc.? Explain why. What are the names of some suitable locations?

Action and Follow-up for Activity #1:

1. The inservice leader should have the recorder present the group responses for each question. Allow the faculty time to discuss if the responses are within the scope of the school or within the teachers' ability to implement in a cost effective manner. Ask the recorder to write these comments on the group paper.

2. The inservice leader should collect all of the group reports and ask the school secretary to type the report and make four copies of each. One copy should be returned to the group, the second copy should be posted on the bulletin board in the faculty lounge, the third copy is for school records, and the fourth copy should be given to an "action committee." The action committee should be established by school officials from volunteers. It is vital that the volunteers include two single parents, a teacher, a counselor, a school social worker or school psychologist, and an assistant principal. The committee must be organized within one week after the inservice group activity and it must be given two weeks to complete all action. The action required is to review all group reports and make recommendations to the school principal on those items that the action committee perceives can be implemented at the school in a cost effective manner. As many specifics as feasible should be delineated to assist the school officials in decision making. Recommended methods of implementations, locations, times, dates, costs, description of activities, suggested persons in charge, etc., should be clearly specified. The action committee must give a copy of the rough draft of the consolidated and revised group reports to the school secretary for typing and forwarding to the inservice leader.

3. The inservice leader should review the final report and discuss it with school officials. Any additional suggestions for implementation should be shared.

Activity #2: Addressing Financial Concerns

What the Inservice Training Leader Should Do:

1. Same as in Activity #1
2. Same as in Activity #1
3. Same as in Activity #1

Rationale for Activity #2:

Single parents oftentimes have difficulty paying school activity and lunch fees for their children, as well as purchasing items such as: sports equipment, instruments for the band, notebooks, or clothing and costumes for activities such as ballets. These parents will become more involved in school if they are assisted in coping with the aforementioned financial problems. Assistance can be in the form of reducing the costs for their children, finding donors to assist in the funding, finding alternatives to the activities themselves, holding the activities in the community or churches where many of the single, African-American parents reside, or by employing school transportation to offset costs. The group task is to share ideas; engender realistic and innovative strategies to improve school involvement by addressing this dire financial situation and to provide a five to ten minute to the faculty.

Procedures for Activity #2:

Prepare group responses for each of the questions. Write five options that you can present to single parents who inform you that they simply don't have sufficient funds to cover the costs of purchasing items critical to school activities. Examples of options are: seeking assistance from the local university's band directors, providing listings of nearby pawn shops and garage sales, sponsoring evening workshops on budgeting, posting job listings, or providing guidance on child support collection procedures. Assistance is provided to many low income students through the Free or Reduced Lunch Program. Should assistance or discounts be given to these students and their parents for school activities such as plays and sporting events? Why or why not? Should local businesses be contacted to provide assistance to low SES single parents and their kids so the activities are more accessible to these parents and students? If so, list some nearby businesses that may be receptive to providing assistance. Are there any school activities that can be conducted in the churches, YMCAs, apartment complexes, recreation centers, and other community agencies in low income neighborhoods? What are the activities and where are the neighborhoods? Identify the churches and community agencies. List the pros and cons of using school transportation to transport students and parents to school activities. Is this feasible for any school activities?

Action and Follow-up for Activity #1: The action will be the same as the action and follow-up for Activity #1.

Activity #3: Insensitivities

What the Inservice Training Leader Should Do:

1. Same as in Activity #1
2. Same as in Activity #1
3. Same as in Activity #1

Rationale for Activity #3:

Children of single parents often feel as if there are no other children of single parents in their classes. Programs that emphasize their adjustment problems frequently leave a negative stigma on the children (Wanat, 1991). For instance, being called out of class to talk with the school counselor may exaggerate the seriousness of a child's problem and call attention to the fact that the child is being raised by one parent. These children sometimes feel that the school fails to recognize their families, especially through communications to the home. For example, letters addressed "To the parents of" assume that both parents reside with the child. Activities such as parents' night or father/son banquets make single-parent children feel uncomfortable.

Procedures for Activity #3:

Prepare group responses for each of the questions. Discuss some statements you heard on the intercom that demonstrated an insensitivity to the feelings of children from single parents homes. What are some statements made in the faculty lounge, cafeteria, and in the hall ways that demonstrated an insensitivity to the feelings of children from single parents homes? List any information posted on the school bulletin boards or school walls that could create a negative stigma for these children. What are some insensitivities that you would suggest to educators to be wary of when mailing bulk correspondence to families? Reflect on the titles of school activities such as the father/son banquet. How many of these activities are there in your school wherein the name or description may indicate an insensitivity to the feelings of single parents' children. What are some alternative methods to rewrite the titles or the descriptions.

Action and Follow-up for Activity #1: The action and follow-up will be the same as the action and follow-up for Activity #1.

Activity #4: Positive Adult Role Models

What the Inservice Training Leader Should Do:

1. Same as in Activity #1
2. Same as in Activity #1
3. Same as in Activity #1

Rationale for Activity #4:

Most single-parent children, particularly boys, need more attention from male adults than other male children. Male students need to spend extra time talking with male adults about their feelings (Morris, 1990).

Procedures for Activity #4:

Prepare group responses for each of the questions. Recall all of the guest speakers that you invited to your classrooms in the previous twelve months. How many were males and how many were females? How many did you invite to stay after the presentation and talk with the male students? Many times single parents' children have a need to express conflicting feelings to someone but don't know how. What are some role-playing or classroom instructional activities that would promote an expression of feelings? How do you feel about asking a male student to share his feelings with a male staff member such as a member of the custodial staff, or a cafeteria worker? Do you think that field trips should be planned to businesses to expose minority male students to successful minority male lawyers, doctors, engineers, etc. What are some businesses in close proximity of the school that you would recommend?

Action and Follow-up for Activity #4:

The action and follow-up will be the same as the action and follow-up for Activity #1.

Activity #5: Non-Custodial Parent Involvement

What the Inservice Training Leader Should Do:

1. Same as in Activity #1
2. Same as in Activity #1
3. Same as in Activity #1

Rationale for Activity #5:

A custodial parent is the one most often viewed by schools as the child's "parent." More often than not, the custodial parent is not the only parental figure in the child's life. Involvement should be encouraged from the custodial and the noncustodial parent in the educational activities of the child. Both should receive report cards and both should be scheduled for conferences with the teacher. A focus of this nature will lead to augmented student academic motivation.

Procedures for Activity #5:

Prepare group responses for each of the questions. Do you feel your school policies encourage school involvement by the noncustodial parent? If not, what are your suggestions? Do your school records keep adequate and current information on the noncustodial parent. If not, describe vital information that should be in the school's database on the noncustodial parent. Share with your group what you have experienced while endeavoring to facilitate communications between the two parents that had a negative influence on you and a negative influence on the motivation of the child. Reflect and discuss if you perceive that you handled the situation appropriately. List seven instances wherein you have extended an invitation to the non-custodial parent to assist with the education of his or her child.

Action and Follow-up for Activity #5: The action and follow-up will be the same as the action and follow-up for Activity #1.

In one study, 65 percent of the parents surveyed felt school administrators still assumed both parents lived at home (Clay, 1981). This reluctance of school administrators to adjust to the changing family is evident in school districts' practices in obtaining information regarding noncustodial parents. Austin (1993) found that in 45 percent of the school districts, the school registration forms did not provide space for the non-custodial parent's name, address, or phone number. When the information was requested, if the custodial parent chose not to provide the information about the non-custodial parent even when no court order existed denying the non-custodial parent's access rights, administrators did not press for such information.

AFRICAN-AMERICAN ALIENATION

To alleviate or eliminate the alienation of many African-American families from public school involvement, initially, it is essential to determine the basis or reasons for alienation. In many cases, the reasons stem from the fact that these families' own problems take precedence over their children's education. However, if the situation involves an abusive environment, the only kind of solution possible may be to refer the parent to an outside agency. Also, some African-American parents are simply not joiners, even though they may care deeply about their children's education. For those that are not joiners, several approaches hold promise. Newsletters with suggestions for home activities have proven to be successful, as have school-based activities where there is "safety in numbers" (for example "make-and-take" workshops and meeting parents on their own turf through home visits) (Greene & Vandegrift, 1992).

All of the schools that I have seen with successful African-American family involvement programs employ myriad and diverse involvement strategies. They are cognizant that the success of any one family involvement strategy depends on how well it matches up with individual family members' needs. The secret is to know who your family members are: assess their needs and talents by employing reliable and valid measures, provide personalized services at the schools with an invitational approach that will adequately address their needs, invite them to come into the school and use their talents, don't coerce them into making long-term commitments to school projects, and show genuine appreciation for their efforts. Below are some general principles that schools can follow to enhance African-Americans involvement in the educational process.

Tips to Enhance Involvement

1. Don't assume you know the families' needs. Assess the needs through interviews, surveys, and conversations with influential persons in the African-American communities. Examples are ministers, deacons, community group leaders, and African-American public school teachers.

2. Get to know African-American families individually. Extend an invitation for them to come and visit the school. Personalize and make the invitation more "inviting" by providing breakfast or lunch in the school cafeteria at no charge.

3. Provide a range of activities to encourage support and participation, including non-threatening, low-commitment opportunities.

4. Personalize home-school communications; making African-American families feel comfortable is an important step toward improving family involvement. Use the phone and face-to-face conferences extensively.

5. Involve African American churches in the recruitment process. Keep the ministers and deacons informed of school programs and activities. Incorporate announcements in the church bulletins.

African-Americans, in particular, have been excluded from primary job opportunities, but the increased complexity of living has put African-American families and children at greater risk today than in the past (Comer, 1987). The risk began its upward spiral after World War II when education became the ticket of admission to good jobs, and television and rapid transportation fragmented the sense of community that once gave support and direction to families. This fragmented sense of community was translated into a lesser focus on the educaion of African-American children as a top priority of African-American families. Additionally, because of their own negative experiences with schools, many African-American parents do not believe the schools sincerely want to educate their children or involve them as partners. They perceive to see the schools as an entity that has betrayed and abandoned them as students and will most likely betray and abandon their children.

The pressures of living in crowded quarters, in neighborhoods where drugs may be a way of life, where temptations for children are everywhere, make it increasingly difficult for parents to get involved in schools and to convince their children that there is hope for the future through education (Swap, 1990). Parents may see schools as unhelpful because they themselves may have experienced failure in school. Such parents often see their children's failure as their own. Time and circumstances may present even interested, concerned parents from participating in the traditional parent organizations (Jackson, Davies, Cooper, & Page, 1988).

Many African-American families feel that schools favor the children of middle income and high income families (Lewis, 1992). This causes the parents/family members negative feelings and a sense of powerlessness. Even when their children attend middle-class schools, their education often continues to be inequitable because of differential learning environments within schools resulting from such phenomena as tracking and teacher expectancy (Eder, 1981). The reaction of low-income and African-American families to the inequitable educational system is alienation (Newman, 1981), perceptions of powerlessness, sense of low control, meaninglessness, cultural estrangement, and feelings of futility and resignation to mediocrity. African-American families suffer passively or express suffering in ways that irritate the larger society. This causes an "us-them" imagery which reduces their desire to join the "other side." They don't perceive themselves as stakeholders with real power. Real power means that all stake holders have a better understanding of what is being done to meet the needs of the students, and they will work together to meet their goals. Another problem the schools will be forced to deal with is one of the most painful social phenomena of our time: this is the deliberate refusal of many African-American children to work up to their capacity. These are not lazy or dumb students but students who are deliberately refusing to achieve. These students are attaching a negative stigma to those Black students who are endeavoring to achieve as "trying to act White." Schools across the country are reporting this attitude among African-American students. The pressure against those youngsters who do their work and try to master their subjects can be overwhelming, whether it takes the form of social ostracism or physical violence. We are watching a whole generation destroy its future. Even some African-American leaders and White liberals have begun to notice this dangerous situation and are alarmed about it. Few are willing to take responsibility for their own role in creating the atmosphere behind such self-destructive attitudes (Sowell, 1992). Schools must address this phenomenon through political action and support groups.

James Comer and many other educators believe that all low SES and minority parents want to and can become involved in the educational activities of their children. James Comer, a Yale University psychiatrist, and his colleagues in several states have been working to reform schools that serve poor and minority children, particularly African-American children (Davies, 1987). Comer believes that, for these schools to be effective, minority parents must play a major role in all aspects of school life, particularly management and governance. He insists on the importance of fostering teacher/student/parent relationships in a democratic setting. In addition, he emphasizes that teachers, families, and specialists must work together to promote the social, emotional, as well as academic growth of children. Schools must implement special strategies to enhance the involvement of African-American parents. Based on the author of this text's extensive interviews with African-American educators and parents, it was found that implementation of the author's "Minority Involvement Model" (MIM) by school administrators will substantially augment African-American parents' participation in the schools and in the classrooms. All items in the MIM are within the capability of most schools to accomplish.

Minority Involvement Model (MIM)

1. Collect information about the immediate needs of the African-American students' families at your school. An analysis of this information should indicate areas of needs that your school can address by providing support services or sponsoring support groups during the evening hours or on the weekends. Examples may be support groups for African-American single parents, working parents, and divorced parents. Additionally, classes facilitated by teachers and counselors on survival skills and parenting skills, or exposing children to cultural activities should be in high demand.

2. Create school plans and seek assistance from local, state, and federal agencies to incorporate many of the skills and abilities of individual African-American parents in the school. This may be on a pay or voluntary basis. A pay basis would consider skills of family members who are carpenters, mechanics, plumbers, or laborers. A voluntary basis would include talents of family members who are dancers, artists, or community leaders. The latter group can assist with the dance club, choir, tutoring, or working with advisory groups in the school.

3. Identify all current school activities with high involvement by African-American families and devise a strategy to communicate this information to the White communities and all minority communities. Solicit help from teachers, custodians, counselors, secretaries, and assistant principals in the schools to "spread the word" by making announcements in their churches, political organizations, and community organizations.

4. Extend an invitation to African-American parents to become involved in the governance of the school. Also, they should have input on decisions concerning responsibilities and information about where to ask for assistance if they are unable to fulfill their duties. School administrators should conduct surveys to determine the kinds of school involve-

ment African-American family members want, and they should include them on committees whose purpose is to seek solutions to problems that affect the school. Creating an atmosphere in which these families feel valued, listened to, and part of the decision-making process may enhance their involvement with the school and their children's education (Austin, 1991).

5. Don't wait until the school year is nearly at the termination point. Talk with African-American family members early in the school year to decide how the home and the school can work together. This will establish an initial warm climate instead of a chilly climate. A warm climate promotes school involvement.

6. Give parents information about how to contact the school. Avoid sending home too much formal communication while underutilizing informal contact. Most African-American parents prefer phone communications and face-to-face communications. Communications through breakfast meetings and parent parties are highly effective. Information can also be disseminated via parent conferences, newsletters, progress reports, and report cards. Schools should be careful not to focus on reporting too much negative information on the conduct and achievement of the children. For example, report cards should include some positive comments about academics or school behavior. Conferences should begin on a positive note, then the problem can be discussed with an attitude of "How can the parent and the teacher work together to solve this problem because it is crucial to the future academic success of the student?"

7. Communicate clearly to family members that high expectations for African-American children in academics and behavior will be mandated from all personnel at the school, including: teachers, administrators, custodians, teaching assistants, volunteer workers, cafeteria workers, and school secretaries. All students will be respected, and it will be expected that students respect their peers and adults. Family members are expected to assist in this endeavor by ensuring their children will complete their school work satisfactorily and on time and by promoting the school values at home.

8. Communicate to the African-American families that the schools' expectations for all teachers are to enforce rules that are consistent and fair with clear disciplinary measures for all students. African-American children, particularly African-American males, should not be singled out for punishment.

9. In meetings with all school parents such as the PTA (Parent-Teachers Association), the school leadership must recognize family demographics and diversity. The school leadership should focus on the concept of ethnic diversity. That is, the needs of all ethnic groups of family members should be represented on the agenda.

10. Give African-American children a sense of belonging through a variety of cocurricular activities. Some of the activities should be cultural based. Schedule activities flexibly and allow a partial participation for children who cannot attend all practices and meetings because of home duties.

SUMMARY

Two groups whose adult family members are underrepresented in school involvement are single parent families and African-American families. If the present trends continue, 60 percent or more of today's children will spend some time in single-parent homes before their eighteenth birthdays. Most of these children will spend as many as six years in homes with only one parent (Sweet & Bumpass, 1988). In the last twenty years, the percentage of African-American children being raised by a grandparent has risen from 3.2 percent to 12.5 percent (or one in eight) (Edwards & Young, 1992). African-American families have unique concerns that need to be addressed. They have been excluded from primary job opportunities, and the increased complexity of living has put African-American families and children at greater risk today than in the past (Comer, 1987). Schools must implement special strategies to enhance the involvement of African-American parents.

Teachers are now in a unique position to provide help and support to single parents, African-American parents, and their children. They can play a significant leadership role in helping parents move through difficult times. They should hold school events at times and places so that these parents can attend. A list of community resources should be provided to help connect adults to community networks. Teachers need to also check out their own personal assumptions about single parents and African-American parents and avoid the use of expressions such as "broken homes," and "low income housing projects." Teachers should know the laws relating to single parents, including parental rights regarding report cards. Report cards and records should be sent to the noncustodial parent. Schools should provide support groups and meetings for single parents and African-Americans during the evening hours or on the weekends. The support groups can be led by a counselor. Child care should be made available to encourage attendance. For example, a local high school's family-life class could set up babysitting while parents attend school functions. School facilities can be used wherein families can band together once a week, and set up their own activities. For example, the group can plan a potluck supper with everyone bringing a covered dish. Movies can follow dinner. Families can plan regular outings such as trips to the African-American cultural center and other cultural events in the city. On weekends, members can take turns babysitting for children in the group.

ACTIVITIES FOR THE READERS

1. Prepare group responses for each of the questions. What are the ten major school and classroom activities you feel that parents should assist with coordinating or should attend? Which of the above would be especially difficult for single parents based on the information in the rationale? Explain why. How can these activities be modified to promote better participation by single parents? For example, would it be feasible to have the activities at night, on the weekends, at a local church, at the YMCA, etc.? Explain why. What are the names of some suitable locations?

2. Collect journals and magazine articles relative to single parent involvement. Only collect those that are current within the last eight years. Identify as many involvement strategies as possible from the journals and magazines and share them with the class.

3. Write five options that you can present to single parents who inform you that they simply don't have sufficient funds to cover the costs of purchasing items critical to school activities. Assistance is provided to many low income students through the Free or Reduced Lunch Program. Should assistance or discounts be given to these students and their parents for school activities such as plays and sporting events? Why or why not? Should local businesses be contacted to provide assistance to low income, single parents and their kids for school activities so that the activities are more accessible to these parents and students? If so, list some nearby businesses that may be receptive to providing assistance. List the pros and cons of using school transportation to transport students and parents to school activities. Is this feasible for all school activities?

4. Write your philosophy of education. Explain it to a low SES parent or family member. What problems did you encounter in explaining it? In what specific ways did they agree or disagree with your philosophy?

5. Discuss some statements you heard on the intercom that demonstrated an insensitivity to the feelings of children from single parents homes. What are some statements made in the faculty lounge, cafeteria, and in the hallways that demonstrated an insensitivity to the feelings of children from single parents homes? List any information posted on the school bulletin boards or school walls that could create a negative stigma for these children. What are some insensitivities that you would suggest to educators to be wary of when mailing bulk correspondence?

6. Interview a teacher and inquire about the guest speakers that were invited to the classroom in the previous six months. How many were males and how many were females? How many were invited to stay after the presentation and talk with the male students? Many times single parents' kids have a need to express conflicting feelings to someone but don't know how. What are some role-playing or classroom instructional activities that would promote an expression of feelings? How do you feel about asking a male student to share his feelings with a male staff member such as a member of the custodial staff, or a cafeteria worker? Do you think that field trips should be planned to businesses to expose minority male students to successful minority male lawyers, doctors, engineers, etc. What are some businesses in close proximity that you would recommend?

7. You are responsible for publicizing a parent/family meeting relating to ways in which the school plans to involve low income and African-American parents. Describe the methods and techniques that you would use in publicizing the meeting.

8. Interview a teacher and record the following information: Do you feel your high school policies encouraged school involvement by the noncustodial parent? If not, what are your suggestions? Do your school records keep adequate and current information on the noncustodial parent? If not, describe vital information on the noncustodial parent that should be in the school's database. Share some problems that you have experienced while endeavoring to facilitate communications between the two parents that had a negative influence on you and a negative influence on the motivation of the child. Reflect and discuss if you perceive that you handled the situation appropriately. List seven instances wherein you have extended an invitation to the noncustodial parent to

assist with the education of his or her child. After you have reviewed the responses for each question, organize the information in the form of a report and share it with your classmates.

Chapter Three

"DEALING WITH TEACHERS' ATTITUDES"

TEACHERS' "BAD ATTITUDES"

Teachers' attitudes concerning pursuing school involvement of low SES and African-American families varies from school to school and teacher to teacher. However, I have interviewed large numbers of teachers who have had negative experiences with endeavoring to get these parents/family members involved in the school process. These negative experiences oftentimes resulted in "bad attitudes" toward school involvement. Prosise (1990) supports the assertion that teachers' negative experiences result in a reluctance to have parents involved in the academic realm of the classroom for several reasons:

1. The classroom is perceived as the teacher's responsibility, and he/she is unwilling to let go. For some teachers who have never had a volunteer from a low SES or African-American family in the classroom, this represents a threatening change.

2. A perception that family members are more inclined to snoop than assist. There is a belief that the information found during the snooping may be distorted and given to the principal or the superintendent.

3. The additional work of training and monitoring the family members may be more trouble than what it is worth. Many teachers are intimidated by their presence because they lack the training necessary to effectively coordinate volunteer services.

4. Teachers may have personal insecurities or may lack confidence in their skills.

5. Teachers believe that the family members are difficult, noisy, or bothersome, so they consciously work to keep them out of their classrooms.

There are additional reasons that "feed" some teachers' negative attitudes toward family involvement. From the teachers' vantage point, many African-American students, and students of low SES parents, come to school socially and academically unprepared, and parents show little practical interest in promoting their learning and social development. Also, many teachers perceive:

1. The parents often feel no identity with regard to their self-worth (Burchard & Burchard, 1987).

2. The parents have little understanding of how their children develop and learn and often lack even the basic information on how to care for children (Edelman, 1987).

3. The parents are often engaged in multiple pathologies such as drug abuse and illiteracy (Burland, 1984).

4. The parents are often extremely pessimistic, lacking any faith that they or their family can improve with planning and effort (Garbarino, 1982).

5. Parents have a personal history that influences their "risk" condition in degrading ways (Nichols, 1990).

These perceptions cause some teachers to label many low income and African-American students as bad children or "poor learners." The teachers perceive themselves as professional baby-sitters and disciplinarians instead of educators. They cease to enjoy their jobs and cease to devote the necessary planning time and energy to ensure the success of the students. It is my contention that when teachers have good attitudes and good experiences concerning family involvement, all persons in the learning milieu of the children will benefit tremendously. When teachers help low SES and African-American family members to help their children, these family members can be as effective with their children as those with more education and leisure time whom teachers expect to help their children. The following are some helpful suggestions to transform "bad attitudes" into "good attitudes."

Suggestions for Teachers

1. Catch Family Members Being Good

The teachers can "catch family members being good" while they are in the school assisting on either a paid or voluntary basis. That is, teachers should make a conscious effort to focus on the good behaviors of the family members and to reinforce those good behaviors with tangible and intangible rewards. The rewards may be certificates, smiley faces, tokens, etc. Take pictures of the parents performing good deeds and post the pictures on the bulletin board. Sign the pictures and give a copy of them to the children to carry home and give to the parents. Videotape the parents in action and let the kids be the live camera crew. Particularly effective is praise given in the presence of other adults, at school wide assemblies, and in the presence of their kids. I have found that this technique of "putting most of the teacher attention on positive behaviors" strengthens those behaviors and causes the negative behaviors to quickly vanish.

Please do not devote most of your attention to the negative behaviors of family members. They are human and will make mistakes. Overdwelling on negative behaviors will result in alienation, reinforcement of the negative behaviors, or the family member quitting the school task. For example, if a family member or parent volunteers to tutor or assist with taking phone calls in the main office, the teacher or school administrator should lavish much genuine praise on the person because he or she took time out from a busy schedule to help the school. This technique will engender a win-win climate and the parent will become an ally. The self-esteem needs of parents and family members can be met when teachers send positive notes home, make positive telephone calls, and make positive comments in public about parents and family members. Self-esteem is degraded when educators constantly invite parents and family members to school only when their children are in trouble.

2. Encourage Interpersonal Skills

It is crucial for low SES and African-American family members to feel welcomed and wanted by the school. The teachers and principal should create a warm environment which encourages and supports family member involvement. A key ingredient in this endeavor is superior interpersonal skills for volunteers. Administrators may want to contact a nearby university to request inservice training from a professor in the College of Business, Human Services, or Education. Many low SES and minority parents are intimidated by teachers. This fear coupled with failures in the school, constant negative notes about the academics and conduct of their children, and the daily pressures of survival will be on the family members' minds when they are conferencing with the teacher. However, showing empathy for their problems, beginning and ending the conversation with positive information about the family member or child, not interrupting the family members while they are talking (good listening skills), and helping them solve their personal and immediate concerns by referral to the appropriate community or government agency, are elements of good interpersonal skills.

Being a good listener and trust-building are two important interpersonal skills to have in every encounter with these parents/family members. People who frequently interrupt, who always have a better story, or who seem to be waiting for the one speaking to breathe so that they can begin to talk, communicate that they are discounting the value of the other person's ideas. Listening attentively and making appropriate responses communicate respect and a genuine appreciation for another. Educators will not receive the trust of these parents/family members by telling them that the educators are trustworthy. Educators need to show a great deal of patience and sincerity. Give the trust enough time to build. Lastly, down play an at-risk label when talking with parents. Teachers should make statements like, "your child is not doing as well as he or she should be doing."

3. Conduct Training

Extremely important is not assigning a family member to a task unless there is a good training program or briefing procedure in place. It is imperative that a training program is in place for all volunteer work, including answering the phone. In this instance, the parent or family member should be allowed to monitor how the secretary answers the phone, the procedures for dialing numbers should be delineated, and the logs or phone message pads should be explained. If the phone message is to be placed in the mailbox then the location of the mailboxes should be shown. This will increase the confidence of the family members. Remember to be careful not to say anything or exhibit any behaviors that convey insensitive messages.

4. Extend an Invitation Early in the School Year

In the beginning of the school year, teachers should contact their students' parents via postcard or telephone. Extend an invitation for them to get involved in school activities. Briefly discuss the major school events for the year and what they can do to assist. Discuss how they can help out in the classroom and at home to increase the successes of the child. Provide them with listings of tutoring sites with phone numbers. When communicating with parents, teachers should reinforce the idea that they are looking forward to working with parents to educate children (Clark, 1989). It should be noted that parents can reinforce education by supporting the school in the home. Be specific as to what your expectations are. Do not wait until the middle of the school year to contact family members. This should be accomplished prior to the start of school or during the first week. Research shows that a paramount reason for the alienation and non-involvement of low SES and minority parents/family members is that they are never extended an invitation to help. Lastly, try to contact parents every ten days regardless of whether the information is good or bad. Many parents become defensive and nervous when the teachers phone them after a lengthy period of time.

5. Create an Open Door Policy

Institute a genuine open-door, open phone policy for actively listening to parental concerns. Encourage them to drop by and observe the class or eat lunch with you. Inform them to phone you if there are any concerns they have about their child or about your classroom. Let them know that teaching is a team effort and a partnership between parents and teachers. Do not take the position that family members are in your class to snoop, find problems, or report them to the principal or superintendent. Family members are allies and want to help. It will take frequent communication and a positive attitude to make the partnership work.

6. Be Cognizant of the Problems of Single Parent Children

Students who have lost parents through divorce or death, will come to class with conflicting thoughts in their minds that need sorting out. Many will have low self-esteem. Teachers can have a tremendous influence on student recovery by giving sincere interest, care, and advice to this situation. This support from teachers will be translated by students and parents into appreciation and trust. The appreciation and trust will facilitate and sustain positive communications between the parent and teacher. Also, for these students, keeping a log or diary will be a very positive activity for exploring feelings, creating meaningful discussions, diagnosing problems, and supplying informal therapy. Students, parents, and other family members will see the writings as an accomplishment in putting ideas and feelings on paper. Much like bibliotherapy, the teachers will gain appreciation for students' dilemmas and can offer assistance or counselor referrals, as needed. Subjects covered in logs could be extended in classroom discussions or other writing exercises. The classroom discussions and writing exercises could also be used as a basis for effective and positive communications with family members (Lewis, 1992).

7. Become a Facilitator for Support Groups

Many family members will not get involved until their immediate needs and unique concerns are addressed. Educators, particularly counselors and social workers, can use their talents and training to serve as coordinators or facilitators for support groups such as teens, single parents, noncustodial parents, grandparents, or working parents. When the family members witness educators volunteering to facilitate support groups, they will be more inclined to volunteer to assist with school activities. They will perceive educators as caring people, sensitive to the real concerns of others.

8. Communicate With Non-custodial Parents

This can be a touchy situation, because oftentimes there are bad emotions existing between the custodial and non-custodial parent. Yet, there are many noncustodial parents who want to assist in the educational activities of their child. This is their right by law and they should not be deprived of that right. Teachers should endeavor to provide both legal and noncustodial parents with regular information about what is going on in the child's classroom, as well as what the parents may need to do to help. Ensure that progress reports, report cards, newsletters, and other information are submitted to both parents. Let them know that you are not taking sides but are doing what is best to maximize the academic success of the child. Empathize with both parents. However, if the situation causes you a tremendous amount of mental frustration, discuss it with your principal. Request that the principal meet with you, both parents, and a counselor to resolve the problem.

9. Turn Parents into Teachers

Educators can create learning activities that parents can use at home with their children. By doing this, teachers are extending the school into the home. However, teachers must provide activities that the family member and the child will have success in completing. The activities should reinforce classroom instruction. They should be brief and fun. Examples are puzzles or brain teasers. It is imperative that the directions are clear. Teachers may need to phone the family members and explain how to complete the activities and how the activities are related to the lesson in the classroom. Also, numerous low SES parents do not know how to answer questions relating to the homework assignments because they are not confident in their abilities to do so. They are not cognizant of any alternatives and simply do nothing.

The teacher should make it explicit that parents should see that the assignment is at least complete, if not correct, each evening. This method is a great opportunity to persuade students to bring some work home, pay attention in class, and communicate with their parents (Hyde, 1991). It is an opportunity for the teacher to respond to parents with statements like, "You don't need to know algebra to help. His teachers do that during class. You just need to see that he does his homework. In fact, it would help him understand it better if you have him explain it to you." This technique usually increases communication between parent and child and teacher and parent. Parents share the feeling of helping the child. Teachers should also provide helpful suggestions to parents which they could use in working with their children at home. For example, teachers can give parents a list of books which parents could read to their children (Jennings, 1992).

10. Conduct Round-Table Discussions

Teachers can meet parents or family members in the gymnasium and hold round-table discussions. They can be required to pick up their students' report card at this event. When this event is planned for the first grading period, it becomes a very successful way to get many low SES and African-American parents/family members to school and open the door for subsequent family member/teacher communications. Be careful not to embarrass family members if their students are failing. They will be very sensitive to negative information about their children's academics in the presence of other parents. Keep the round-table discussion brief. Also, the discussions will be more effective if the teacher establishes and maintains an informal and relaxed atmosphere. This can be accomplished by serving light refreshments such as punch, cookies, doughnuts, coffee, and sandwiches. Lastly, it should be requested that parents dress in casual attire.

11. Initiate an "Informational Card" System

Teachers can institute an "Informational Card" system. Cards can be printed with school information on the front. Leave space on the back of the card to write a positive message about a family member of a student in their class. This could be information about talents, hobbies, job promotions, community achievements, etc., of the family member. Every teacher must send at least one card per week. Return cards to the office, where they can be stamped and mailed. The idea is to target family members who you want to be more active in school activities through praise for some recent accomplishment. The accomplishment may or may not be school related. I have seen this to be more effective when family members' pictures are put on the card. All adults and children like to see their name and picture in a media that has a wide circulation.

12. Visit Families On Their Turf

Go to the homes of the families. There are several benefits to doing this. Teachers can gain an appreciation of the culture of the child, and parents have more respect for teachers who are not fearful of visiting low SES housing. However, for the first two visits, I recommend considering going with another teacher, counselor, or social worker. If a good rapport is established with a parent, ask the parent to assist you on future visits. Additionally, show up at the local churches, community centers, and other meeting places and share information with the low SES and minority families on how to assist the teacher in the educational development of their children. At the meetings request that parents who are participating in the school invite other parents to participate. Extend an invitation to all family members to attend school activities.

13. Consider Work Schedules

Many parents will not show up for school conferences because of conflicts with work. Stagger conference times to accommodate parents' work schedules as best as possible. Talk major employers into letting parents have time off to attend conferences. Consider holding conferences at night and on the weekends. Educators may also want to hold conferences at a facility in the community that is in close proximity to the family member.

14. Combine Business Meetings With School Activities

Family members enjoy seeing their child on stage performing in plays or participating in sports such as basketball or football. Teachers can capitalize on family members' proclivity to be present in large numbers at these functions to observe their children. Phone parents and encourage them to come and see their child perform. This is an excellent opportunity to hold a small business meeting, but limit the meeting to about twenty minutes and hold the meeting at the beginning of the school activity.

15. Awareness of Enabling by Parents/Family Members

Enabling is a term associated with support groups such as Alcoholics Anonymous. It means cushioning people from the effects of poor choices. This fosters dependency and perpetuates self-defeating behaviors. Educational enabling is when parents/family members take the responsibility for the procrastination, laziness, and irresponsibility of their children. These are parents who do homework or other projects for a child who procrastinates or gets frustrated easily. These parents call school to excuse a child for being tardy or skipping classes, pressure teachers to give the child higher grades than were earned, and consistently ask administrators or counselors to intervene to solve the students' problems. They are letting their children off the hook. Educators should inform parents/family members of the ills of educational enabling. Parents and teachers should prepare students with experiences and skills that prepare them to cope with both the rough and smooth air of life. Educators can introduce parents/family members to the concept of enabling and discuss why it isn't good for the children. Educators can request that parents/family members think two or three times before they bail students out of school related problems. Low SES and minority students need to learn how to deal with conflict and challenges (Landfried, 1991).

16. Conduct Effective Parent-Teacher "Problem-Oriented" Conferences

Most parent-teacher conferences are scheduled to discuss a problem or find a solution to the child's difficulties (Welch & Tisdale, 1986). Therefore, the teacher should be well prepared. Examples of the child's work and significant test results should be available at the conference. Prepare several constructive solutions to the problem. If a new teacher is conducting the conference, he/she should ask for suggestions from veteran teachers and administrators about what to say and how to act. Always begin the conference with positive information about the parent/family member and child. Remember that the parent wants the child to achieve and behave in your classroom as much as you do. Use the word we rather than I to demonstrate to the parent that the solution to the problem is a joint effort of two equal partners, the teacher and the parent. Problem conferences have no set duration; the typical minimum allotment will be about twenty minutes.

Be cautious about inviting too many school personnel to attend the conference such as administrators, counselors, and the school psychologist. This may result in the parent feeling outnumbered and part of an easily outvoted minority (Mcloughlin, 1987). Encourage the parent to bring a friend such as a minister, deacon, or family friend for support, if he/she feels the need to do so. Because of the emotion and complexity involved in this type of conference, additional conferences may need to be scheduled to arrive at a satisfactory solution. Try not to allow the game of "passing the buck" to occur. This is when the teacher will say the problem is the fault of the previous year teacher or the previous school. The parent may say the problem is the fault of the non-custodial parent, illness, or a learning disorder. The teacher should be calm, open, frank, and should refrain from talking in generalities and using educational jargon. Be very specific in stating the problem and try to arrive at a solution that is agreeable to the parent. Do not make hurtful statements or be defensive. The teacher should remember that the best decisions are made based on cooperation with the parent and analyzing the facts rather than on emotions. Remember that it takes at least two persons to argue. Complete my "Problem-Oriented Conference Checklist" several days prior to the parent-teacher conference date.

Problem-Oriented Conference Checklist

Summary of the Specific Problem or Difficulty the Child is Having

_____

_____

_____

Date, Time, Location, and Approximate Length of the Conference

_____

_____

Additional School Personnel Who Should Attend

_____

Additional Personnel the Parent Should Ask to Attend

_____

Pertinent Background Information on the Parent (Single Parent, Hobbies, Interests, Other Members in the Household, Significant Family Problems, Employment Hours, etc.)

_____

_____

_____

Summary of Pertinent Grade, Attendance, and Behavior Information

_____

_____

_____

_____

Summary of Positive Information Teacher Will Say About the Parent and Child at the Beginning and End of the Conference

_____

_____

_____

Summary of Questions to ask

_____

_____

Proposed Solutions that will be Shared at the Conference

_____

_____

_____

Other Important Information to Remember

_____

_____

_____

Teachers Interviewing for Talents

All low SES and African-American parents and family members are talented. These talents can be used as a basis for enhancing school involvement. Parents do not have to come to the school to work with their child or to work in the class of their child. Many parents get a tremendous amount of satisfaction from helping other children. Use the parents/family members' talents in a productive manner. Initially, the teacher must ascertain what the talents are by surveying parents or through phone interviews. Below are open ended questions that can be used in the interview and survey process. Teachers can use all of the questions, select from the Sixteen questions those that might benefit their school or classroom, or modify the questions as needed. If the teacher decides to employ the survey method, some of the questions can quickly be converted to a Likert scale to significantly reduce the time for the parent/family members to complete the survey.

Parent/Family Interview or Survey Model

1. What job do you currently hold?

2. What jobs have you held in the previous 5 years? Would you be interested in being invited to speak before a class or a small group of students to discuss your job?

3. What times during the day would you be available to assist in the classroom or in the school?

4. What are your hobbies and interests? Teachers are always looking for talented parents such as firemen, carpenters, barbers, etc., to share their talents with the class. Are you interested?

5. What sports have you played or coached? Would you be willing to demonstrate and talk about sports during a class or school activity?

6. What type of music do you prefer? Would you be willing to play music and talk about music during a class or school activity?

7. List three of your favorite songs. List three of your favorite singers. Can you sing? Would you be willing to sing during a parent talent day or be a disc jockey for a student dance?

8. What types of books do you like to read? List the last three books that you have read. Are you interested in reading stories to just elementary students?

9. Do you have a tape player at home? If so, would you be willing to read a story on tape for use in class?

10. List three successful social events that you have had a significant role in coordinating. Examples may be family reunions, church functions,

Thanksgiving or Christmas parties, etc. Would you be interested in coordinating a similar social event at the school?

11. Have you any experience at tutoring, counseling or teaching in the Church (Sunday School), on your job, or in the community? If so, would you like to volunteer to perform those functions in the classroom?

12. Can you sew or cut out materials? Would you be interested in making bulletin boards in your home for use at the school?

13. Are you in a leadership position on your job or in your community? If the answer is yes, you may be a perfect candidate to assist in parent recruitment from your community. What do you think?

15. Do you know or work with any community leaders, businesspersons or professionals who might volunteer their time and talents to come to the school and serve as tutors, role models, or guest speakers? Please list their names and phone numbers. Would you be willing to assist in coordinating this project?

16. Have you traveled to a country outside the United States? If so, what country? Would you be willing to talk about the country to a class?

When the teacher has collected data from the surveys and has discovered the resources available through the parent/family members, he/she must then consider ways in which these skills, interests, etc., can be used in the school or in the classroom. For example, a parent may have an interest in music or basketball. The parent with the interest in music may be referred to the assistant principal to assist with any musical event that will occur at the school in the near future. The parent with an interest in basketball may be assigned as a counselor or mentor for underachieving students who are on the basketball team or who are involved in the YMCA youth basketball league. The rationale is that students are more responsive to adults with whom they perceive a common bond or connection. Basketball talk will be the connection or the starting point in assisting the students in sorting out priorities. For each parent or family member who completes the questions, the teacher should ask himself or herself, "How can I use the talents of this parent/family member to most effectively get him or her involved in the education of the children in our school?" Even parents who reveal that they have no time to come to the school can perform important school involvement tasks at home. For instance, a parent can recite a poem on tape and the teacher can play the tape in the classroom. However, it is vital that on the tape, the parent preface the poem with a statement similar to the one below:

"This poem is being recited by Mr. Paul Jones. Mr. Paul Jones is the proud father of a student at Quail Hollow Middle School."

A parent who assists by making a bulletin board or a painting at home should have his or her "stamp" on the bulletin board in big letters. An example of a statement that the parent could write proudly in large letters at the lower right corner of the bulletin board is:

"This bulletin board was created by and in the home of Mr. Paul Jones. Mr. Paul Jones is the proud father of a student at Garinger Elementary School."

Signature of Parent or Family Member

After collection of the data employing the "Parent/Family Interview or Survey Model," the next step is for the teacher to extend an invitation to assist with school activities using the "Parent/Family Opportunities Survey." Teachers can use all of the survey items, select from the fourteen items those that might benefit their school or classroom, or modify the items as needed to fit the school and classroom situations. To ensure a good return rate on the survey forms include popcorn, pizza, balloons, or cookies and ice cream parties for the class with the best return rate. Once the parent/family member has consented to participate in the school activities, it is vital that parents are trained or briefed prior to being assigned the task. This will boost their confidence and augment the probability of a successful experience. Developing a core leadership group among the parents will help keep the program active.

If a teacher has several volunteers to choose from, it would be prudent to informally interview parents and select the ones who would work best for that particular situation. The planning and interviewing for volunteers initially requires more work. However, after the initial two or three weeks, volunteers will be more effective and used more efficiently the remainder of the year. Gestures of appreciation are helpful in promoting volunteer work. Parent volunteer luncheons and coffees are examples of ways in which a school can express its gratitude to volunteers. In many instances, low SES and African-American parent/family members, do not become involved in school activities because they are not extended an invitation to assist in an area that they are comfortable with and an area in which they have considerable talent or experience. The "Parent/Family Opportunities Survey" will remedy this situation.

Parent/Family Opportunities Survey

Directions: Thanks for responding to my earlier interview/survey questions. This survey will only take a few minutes to complete. It is an "invitation" for you to use your talents and expertise to get more involved in the school in an area that you feel comfortable with. Please complete this survey and return it to the school in the enclosed self-addressed envelope. You will be contacted for a briefing or training session prior to assignment to an activity.

1. I would prefer speaking to classes.

   Yes _____   No _____

2. I would prefer speaking to the entire student body.

   Yes _____   No _____

3. I would prefer duplicating teachers' materials.

   Yes _____   No _____

4. I would prefer tutoring.

   Yes _____   No _____

5. I would prefer counseling students with low self-esteem.

   Yes _____   No _____

6. I would prefer chaperoning a field trip/party.

   Yes _____   No _____

7. I would prefer monitoring the halls/grounds.

   Yes _____   No _____

8. I would prefer creating bulletin boards.

   Yes _____   No _____

9. I would prefer assisting in the computer lab.

   Yes _____   No _____

10. I would prefer helping in the library.

    Yes _____   No _____

11. I would prefer serving on advisory committees.

    Yes _____   No _____

12. I may be available to assist during

8 to 10 A.M. _____   10 A.M. to 12 P.M. _____

1 to 3 P.M. _____   Some Saturdays _____

Some Evenings _____   Some Nights _____

13. I would like to read books to elementary students.

Yes _____   No _____

14. I would like to share my experiences about a foreign country.

Yes _____   No _____

Many African-American, low SES families feel they have nothing to offer the public schools. By capitalizing on the data from the "Parent and Family Opportunities Survey," teachers will be sending vivid signals that parents/families can contribute, they are talented, and they are a significant part of the educational process. Parents and family members will feel a sense of pride in the school because they are making a contribution in an area in which they feel comfortable. The teacher will have a good attitude toward the parents because their jobs will be made easier. Teachers simply don't have enough time to do bulletin boards and provide the one-on-one counseling that numerous students need.

The two models can be beneficial in another important way. They will make the classroom "come alive" and provide many "real life" experiences that a substantial number of low SES and African-American students don't have. Most of these students have very limited access to enrichment experiences. School budgets and time constraints usually allow few field trips. The models will be more effective if funds are used from a source such as Chapter I funds to hire a parent coordinator for the project, if the school employs a mass mailout, if all information goes into a central database, and if the talents of the family members are reviewed quarterly at faculty meetings and are posted in the teachers' lounges.

To enhance effectiveness of the two models, teachers should review all curriculum materials early in the school year prior to administering the models. Identify topics in the textbooks that will allow you to bring in someone who will make the subject come alive for the students. If the class is studying about a foreign country, locate a parent or family member who has been in that foreign country as a result of military travels or other travels. Another option is that a parent/family member may work with someone from that country or may know someone in the neighborhood who is from Vietnam, China, Japan, Mexico, etc. Instead of having the students only read about Mexico from the text, invite somebody into the classroom to talk about Mexico and show pictures, videos, photo albums, etc. Math, Science, History, and Language Arts texts offer unlimited opportunities for such classroom activities. Due to limited real life experiences, many rural, low SES and African-American students become bored with the textbook because they don't have the experiences to make a connection with many of the words and figures in print. Yet, a student who is stimulated through the written page, as well as the visible world, will have a much better chance of escaping from his/her limited world. As teachers stretch the horizons of the students, they will also contribute to stretching the horizons of the parents' world.

Families as Self-Esteem "Builders" and Tutors

Many low SES and minority family members can be used effectively by teachers as self-esteem "builders" and tutors for underachieving and unmotivated students in the classroom. An equal focus should be placed on self-esteem and tutoring. Both are vital in enhancing achievement. Many of the students' self-esteems have been damaged significantly by numerous adults and peers in and outside of school for many years. The damage has been accomplished by a myriad of diverse negative messages telling the students that they "can't learn," have little self-worth, or are not college material. The numerous academic failures further reinforce the feelings of low self-worth. These students will not achieve until their self-esteem is enhanced. Teachers are usually very busy in the classroom and do not have time to devote the one-on-one attention required to enhance self-esteem. When the student feels good about him/herself, the mind will be more receptive to absorbing content information, and achievement will increase significantly. Low SES and minority families can be vital in this effort.

Teachers need to be careful not to endeavor to get a long term commitment but to concentrate on short term commitments. This is because many of these family members are simply unable to sustain long term commitments. To maximize their effectiveness as tutors, the parents/family members should undergo a brief training program before they are allowed to work with the students. This will augment their successes and give them more confidence in their abilities to carry out the task.

I have found the parents/family members to be more effective when they are allowed to work with individual students instead of with students in small groups. This is because working with small groups requires an extensive amount of training and commitment. It is difficult for them to handle too many misbehavior problems at one time. When small groups are coerced on them, they become frustrated after a brief period and will be reluctant to continue assisting the teacher. They should tutor students who are not related to them and that have no serious misbehavior problems. Involving these parents/family members will lead to greater public support of the public schools and better dropout prevention efforts. Again, it is crucial that families are trained and the training is brief, effective, organized, and emphasizes self-esteem enhancement. Below is a Self-Esteem "Builders" and Tutors Training Model that I have developed specifically for use in the training of parents/family members. There are five steps in the model.

Five-Step Training Model

Step #1: Advertise for Assistance

Rationale for Step #1:

1. Getting parents/family members of low SES and African-American children involved in the school will take an aggressive marketing effort. It is essential that talents and ideas from key players are included in the marketing scheme. The key players should be selected from the following: school administrators, counselors, school social workers, parents from low SES backgrounds, and teachers. Programs are more effective when there is shared leadership among all groups. A sense of ownership is perceived and support for the program is enhanced.

What to Do in Step #1:

1. A committee of approximately seven school personnel should be formed. I recommend the following: an assistant principal, a school counselor, school social worker, two parents from a low SES background, and two teachers. The committee's tasks are to prepare a flyer and disseminate information to the public. The flyer should be prepared similar to the sample below, **Volunteer for Self-Esteem Builders and Tutors Flyer.** The flyer should briefly address five areas: job description, duties, qualifications, time commitment, and benefits. It should appear on the school's letterhead paper to show a clear connection with the school and to look more professional. Disseminate the flyer to community leaders such as ministers, local officials, etc. Additionally, post the flyers in

places frequently visited by the parents. Examples would be fitness centers, grocery stores, YMCAs, apartment buildings, laundromats, community centers, and popular restaurants. Ensure a phone number and the name of a contact person is on the flyer. A school counselor, a school social worker, or the school secretary should be listed as the contact person.

2. The contact person needs to maintain a log of names, phone numbers, and "best times to contact." The contact person should make this information available to the committee on a monthly basis. The committee should share the information with all teachers during faculty meetings.

3. Teachers should become familiar with the training program, phone the family member during the "best times to contact" and invite the parent to come in for a three hour training session. In the training session, the teacher should begin by making the family member feel at ease. This can be done by smiling, acting very warmly to them, making direct eye contact, and expressing thanks for taking time out of their busy schedule to assist the children. Next, a copy of the flyer should be presented to and reviewed with the parent/family member. Each of the five areas should be discussed: Job Description, Duties, Qualifications, Time Commitment, and Benefits.

Volunteer for Self-Esteem "Builders" and Tutors Flyer Wanted!!!!!!!!!!!!!!!!!!!!!!

Parents and Family Members of Students at Quail Hollow Middle School are Needed To Volunteer as Self-Esteem "Builders" and Tutors

Contact the School at the Phone Number 547-4500 and Ask for the Counselor

Job Description:

Parents and family members will provide support to students by tutoring them in a subject in which the parents/family members feel comfortable. They will counsel students to help them resolve personal problems, and to enhance their self-esteem through a supportive attentive relationship.

Duties:

1. Check in at the central office with the school's secretary and sign the designated log at the beginning of each tutoring session.

2. Phone the school as soon as feasible if unable to honor the scheduled tutoring appointment or if delayed in arriving at school.

3. Tutor a student one hour/week during school hours.

4. Contact the student's teachers at least once per month and endeavor to attend the quarterly tutor/teacher breakfast meeting.

5. Phone parents at least once per month.

Qualifications:

1. A love for children.
2. A desire to make a difference in the lives of children.
3. A belief that all students want to and can succeed.
4. Completion of the three hour training session.

Time Commitment:

1. Volunteer one day/week during school hours.
2. Participate in three hours of training time.
3. Attend the quarterly tutor/teacher breakfast meeting (the meeting will last about one hour).

Benefits:

1. Train in empowerment, active listening, behavior modification, and parenting skills.
2. Feel satisfaction from helping a student succeed in school.
3. Gain in the area of interpersonal skills.
4. Learn basic empathy skills.

Step #2: Warm and Supportive Relationship

Rationale for Step #2:

Establishing a warm and supportive relationship and building a positive rapport with the student is vital in enhancing the self-esteem and academic success of the students. Low achieving students need teachers and tutors who genuinely care for them as human beings, respect their feelings, and are concerned about improving their chances for future successes. Even though they may have academic deficiencies, all students are talented in some fashion and have hobbies and experiences they value. Many low SES children are street smart and can readily sense a phony or pretentious adult.

What to Do in Step #2:

1. Emphasize to the family member to be relaxed and be themselves. Inform them that students are quick to detect a phony.

2. Tell the family member that personal concern for the student is one of the greatest assets in promoting self-esteem and effective tutoring. They must work hard to build a relationship of mutual confidence with their students. They must be a good role model at all times, even in the cafeteria, hallways, and entering and leaving the school premises. This is because students will always be watching. Conflicts in "do as I say" or "do as I do" will confuse the students. If the family member is teaching respect to the student but then disrespects a teacher in the cafeteria, the student will lose respect for the family member and self-esteem will be damaged. Adults' behaviors at all times in the presence of students send powerful messages to these students.

3. Provide the family member with the name of the student as well as a nickname. Encourage them to learn it prior to working with the student. Also, the teacher should write down the name of the family member and give it to the student. Students are often hesitant to communicate with tutors when they are uncertain of names.

4. Discuss the student's after school interests, hobbies, and the sports in which they like to participate. Tell the family member that to build rapport, he/she must talk with the student about the student's interests, hobbies, and sports. Ask him or her questions about these activities. Then, listen to the student and try not to interrupt while he or she is talking.

Step #3: A Successful First Session

Rationale for Step #3:

Many of the students that the family member will work with have not had many successes, particularly with adult sponsored programs. It is vital that the initial session with the student is successful to get the student receptive to future sessions. Critical to accomplishing this is incorporating specific strategies to set the stage for success. Tutors must be made aware of specific academic weaknesses, behavioral problems, the need to not give the student the answer, and maintaining records of improvement.

What to Do in Step #3:

1. Review with the tutor all background information in the student's folder very carefully concerning weakness in academics, family problems, and self-esteem problems.

2. Discuss with the tutor the need to begin tutoring at a level well within the grasp of the student. This will provide an atmosphere of success. Tutors should be reminded that the student has had little success in school. Tell them to praise the student for his/her successes, regardless of how small they are because all of the successes are important.

3. Emphasize the need to provide immediate feedback concerning whether the student's answers are right or wrong. The student should clearly know when the tutor is pleased with a right answer. If the student is wrong, the tutor should not show disapproval, but look at the mistake as a challenge.

4. Give the tutor a tablet and show the tutor how to maintain a chart of the student's individual progress. The chart should be submitted weekly to the student's teacher for review.

Step #4: Tutoring Tips From Peers

Rationale for Step #4: Experience and peers are valuable in the training process. New tutors will be more confident when they get advice from successful peers. That is, a tutor who has been through the process and experienced a great deal of success.

What to do in Step #4: The teacher should identify a low SES parent or minority parent who has functioned effectively as a tutor and have the parent review the list of tips with the prospective tutor. The parent should give a copy of the tips to the prospective tutor for future reference. These are tips that parents/family members who were tutors have found to be effective in enhancing tutoring success.

Tips For Tutoring and Self-Esteem Enhancement From Successful Parent/Family Tutors

1. The less work you do for your student the better. Although it is quicker, easier, and less frustrating for a tutor to do a problem or an assignment, it is of little permanent help to the student. Help the student learn how to do the work. Emphasize what the student does right instead of what he or she does wrong.

2. A good tutor will spend most of the time asking questions, listening, and helping the student to think for him/herself, rather than lecturing to the student. Do not set goals so high that the chance of failure prevents the child from trying.

3. Don't expect your student to show appreciation for your efforts.

4. Don't be quick to label or judge. Many of the students you will tutor have had negative stigmas and negative labels attached to them for years. Our goal is not to reinforce these items but for them to gradually overcome them by providing successes.

5. Many of the characteristics which make your student different from you are what makes him an individual. Viewed this way, the student's differences often appear as strengths.

6. Do not talk to the student in a patronizing manner. The student is a human being and all human beings need respect. Set a good example for the student by being courteous and respectful. Think of working with your student, rather than talking at him/her. Make the student feel that he or she belongs. Treat the student as you would like to be treated.

7. Learn the student's name and pronounce it correctly. Learn nicknames, if any; write your name for the student.

8. Be quick to compliment the student on his/her interests, dress, haircut, etc. This will make the student feel good about him/herself and self-esteem will be enhanced. Say something positive to the student each day.

9. Let the student know you are human, too. Admit it when you make a mistake.

10. Use your voice well. Speak softly and slowly. Add variety to your speech. Make direct eye contact with the student and don't distance yourself.

11. Be prepared: have all materials ready. The student will think you're not interested if you are not prepared.

12. Look for ways to motivate your student by involving the student in the activities and by being creative and imaginative in your tutoring methods.

13. Before beginning an explanation of the problem, do not inform the student that "this is an easy problem." If the student encounters significant difficulty working the problem, his/her self-esteem will suffer.

14. You will not be expected to know how to work all problems. Ask the teacher for help if you have a problem that you don't feel you can

handle. Also, answer your child's questions openly, honestly, and immediately, if possible.

15. Don't embarrass the child, especially in front of others; do not make the child question his or her worth.

16. Encourage your student to be proud of his or her name, ideas, and work. Compliment him/her when possible on creative ideas, improvement in performing tasks, etc.

17. Try to see that your student achieves success in some way each day by offering a variety of activities. Give the child recognition for the effort the child makes even though it may not meet up to expectations.

Step #5: Self-Esteem Tips From Peers

Rationale for Step #5:

Experienced peers are valuable in the training process. New self-esteem "builders" will be more confident when they get advice from successful, peer self-esteem "builders." That is, a self-esteem builder who has been through the process and experienced a great deal of success.

What to Do in Step #5:

The teacher should identify a low SES parent or minority parent who has functioned effectively as a self-esteem "builder" and have the parent review the list of tips with the prospective self-esteem "builder." The parent should give a copy of the tips to the prospective self-esteem "builder" for future reference. These are tips from parents/family members that were successful in enhancing self-esteem.

Tips For Self-Esteem Enhancement From Successful Parent/Family Self-Esteem "Builders"

Praise enhances self-esteem for adults and children. There are some phrases depicting praise that are more effective than others. When you want to praise a student for efforts and successes, the focus should be on giving the student genuine praise, immediate praise, and specific praise. Praise the student immediately after the significant effort or the success has occurred. Do not use words or phrases such as "good," "O.K., that's correct," and "very good." Instead, with a look of joy on your face and with pride and enthusiasm, say one of the phrases delineated below. If you do, you boost the student's self-esteem and witness a student who has become more receptive to your tutoring. Accompanying each of the statements below should be a smile, pat on the back, or a hug to increase the effectiveness of the statement.

1. That's great John, you demonstrated that you know the rule!

2. That's quite an improvement Sue, you worked 80 percent of the problems on the worksheet correctly as compared to 60 percent on yesterday's worksheet!

3. Keep it up Gary, I see you attempted to work all of the problems on your worksheet this time, whereas, last time you only attempted to work 30 percent of the problems!

4. It's a pleasure to teach when you work like this! Your work is so organized!

5. What neat work! It is great that you went to the extra effort to do your project paper on a word processor so that it would look better!

6. I'll bet your mom and dad would be proud to see that you finished the entire quiz this time because of the many practice problems you completed the previous two days!

7. I appreciate your work! You were not asked to work the two "Brain Teasers" problems, but you did!

8. Thank you for sitting down, being quiet, etc.!

9. That looks like it is going to be a great report! You followed the directions very well!

10. Very Creative! Your painting has a lot of meaning!

11. Now you've got the hang of it! Simply follow the rule!

12. You've got it now! See the advantage of practice and more practice!

13. You make it look easy when you focus on being organized and writing neatly so that mistakes are readily evident!

14. Now you've figured it out! See how, sometimes, you have to change to a different strategy to get the answer!

15. That's a very good observation! I am elated that you are now checking your work for mistakes!

SUMMARY

Some teachers have a difficult time working with low income and African-American students, partly due to misperceptions that oftentimes lead to poor attitudes and poor behaviors concerning family involvement. In some cases, these teachers have not associated with these types of families in any manner; therefore, they become frustrated when initial endeavors at involvement strategies do not work. My recommendation is for these teachers to use some of my suggestions, undergo some reflective thinking about their beliefs relative to the families, and to extend an invitation early in the school year. It is important to realize that many of the parents do not have all of the middle class values that are ingrained in most schools. Do not let this be a source of mental anguish but accept them as they are. Teachers must be sensitive to the possible limitations of their orientation toward parents as it may have evolved within a mechanistic, deficit, oriented system (Fantini, 1982).

All parents are concerned about the welfare of their children. All parents are talented and want to be treated as partners. Teachers and parents must have a sense of respect for each other's integrity, for their abilities to grow and develop in positive ways as individuals and within their respective roles (Young Children, 1990). Find out about the talents of the parents and family members and provide support systems to assist them in using these talents in the school. Always begin your communications with the families early in the school year. Be sure to make positive comments about the parents and their children, regardless of whether the comments are about academics, clothing attire, or behavior. It takes a conscious effort and a talented teacher to "catch kids and parents being good." Always begin and end every conversation on a positive note. Provide children and family members with a clear idea of how your class works, and encourage parents to become a part of your classroom. Opening meetings with parents should be personal, warm, and inviting, offering them opportunities to get to know you as a person who cares about children. Employing the information in this chapter will engender a warm and supportive relationship with family members which will establish the foundation for effective, long-term partnerships.

ACTIVITIES FOR THE READERS

1. Go to a nearby school and request to see all discipline referrals for the prior month and a listing of student data to include ethnicity, gender, free or reduced lunch list information, etc. Organize this information into a research report. In this report develop a table to depict the number of discipline referrals received by each ethnic group, income group, and gender group. Discuss this data relative to teachers' labeling students as bad children or poor learners, and teachers' perceptions that they are professional "baby-sitters" and disciplinarians instead of educators.

Do your findings support the need for serious efforts to get family members highly visible in the public schools? Why or Why not? What other inferences can you make from the data that will have some educational significance?

2. A suggestion was made by the author that teachers should "catch family members being good" while they are in the school assisting on either a paid or voluntary basis. What is meant by this phrase? Research the terms proactive management and positive reinforcement. Compare and contrast "catch family members being good," proactive management, and positive reinforcement.

3. Interview six principals or assistant principals. They should be from an urban high school, rural high school, urban middle school, rural middle school, urban elementary school, and a rural elementary school. Prepare a report for your class around these questions: What support groups are using the building that have a substantial number of low SES or minority parents? What times do they meet? Where in the school do they meet? Who is the coordinator or facilitator for the group? What is the extent of involvement from school personnel? How long have the support groups been meeting at the school? The support groups that you are targeting are those that are formed to meet immediate and unique needs of groups such as single parents, non-custodial parents, grandparents, and working parents.

4. Go to a nearby school and ask the teacher if you can design an "Informational Card" system for the class. Ensure to put positive notes about several parents and their kids on the cards. Include your picture on the card. Request that the school office mail the cards to the homes of the parents/family members. You should interview the teacher about ten days later and find out the response from the parents whom you have targeted with the positive information. Share this information with the class.

5. All low SES and African-American parents and family members are talented. Locate a class with a substantial number of low SES and African-American students. Ask the teacher if you can ascertain the talents of the parents by surveying parents or through phone interviews using the "Parent/Family Interview or Survey Model." Also, follow up with the "Parent/Family Opportunities Survey." You can use all of the questions or modify the questions as needed. Share this information with the teacher in the form of a report.

6. What is meant by using family members as Self-Esteem "Builders"?

Write down as many statements as possible that you have heard educators and parents say to children that were hurtful to the self-esteem of these students. Why do you think the statements were made? Many students will come into your classroom with low self-esteem. Discuss any classroom activities, classroom procedures, or any behaviors you will model that should enhance their self-esteem.

Chapter Four

SCHOOL ADMINISTRATORS AND INVOLVEMENT

PRINCIPAL'S ROLE IS A CATALYST

The issue of the fragile connection between low SES and African-American families and the schools is a serious one. Efforts can be made by school administrators to make this connection more smooth and secure, and to decrease parents' alienation. This should be high on the agendas of all principals because family involvement is found to directly effect student achievement.

A child's education begins at birth. Parents and family members as their paramount teachers, play an important role in the intellectual, social, and emotional growth of their children. All parents/families and educators must make family involvement in education a priority. The foundation for a successful home-school partnership is effective communication which encourages the development of mutual support between home and school. Parent/families and educators must effectively communicate and join forces to make sure children are successful learners. There are many studies that point to higher achievement when parents/families participate in school activities, monitor children's homework, and otherwise support the extension into the home of the work and values of the schools. Schools cannot operate in a vacuum. They need the support of all families.

Principals must lead the crusade to bring parents/families of low SES and African-American students into the school, not just as passive participants or volunteers, but as full partners between the parent/families and the professional (Sandfort, 1987). Establishing this partnership will not be easy, accustomed as some educators have been to excluding parent participants in any form. The principal's role is that of a catalyst in developing an orientation and an attitude for positive participation. Some suggestions to accomplish this are delineated in this chapter. I am aware that school administrators will be unable to implement all of the suggestions given below. However, school administrators should be capable

71

of implementing some of the suggestions. Implementing only a few should yield significant dividends that will be reflected in enhanced student motivation and achievement.

Suggestions For School Administrators

1. Admit That Help is Needed

This should be the starting point for obtaining school involvement from low SES and African-American families. Go in their communities and let them know that you want and need their help. Publicize this information in the minority newspaper. Do not take this plea as a sign of weakness or incompetence. It takes the entire village to educate kids properly. Don't be afraid to admit that help is needed. The futures of our students are at stake.

2. Implement a Variety of School Involvement Strategies

To best utilize school and family resources, principals must re-think how they respond to the needs of low income and African-American children. Principals should establish school policies that encourage involvement in a variety of ways based on families' talents and interests. In order to do this, certain assumptions must be made by school administrators. These assumptions must be ingrained in the school environment: family members are highly talented, family members care about the future success of their kids, and family members will become involved through the creative efforts of school personnel. School improvement plans should tap the talents of parents (i.e., construction, landscaping, etc.).

Principals need to tailor policy to local need. They should consider the complex family structures and special needs of certain types of families such as single parent families, families with stepparents, families headed by the grandmother, and families where both parents work full time and part time jobs. Principals must examine these local situations and tailor school policies, procedures, and activities to be reflective of the uniqueness of the situations. Additionally, principals need to sponsor adult support groups that are open to all family members. The school's sponsorship might come in the form of free building use, and in the form of exchanging appropriate information to facilitate the group's work. Administrators should employ classroom teachers as effective, specialist facilitators of parent involvement. Support should be given to classroom teachers to accomplish this. Lastly, school administrators should budget money for additional substitutes so that teachers can make home visits.

3. Establish Support Groups for Children

Every school should have a support group for children from divorced or separated families to help these young people cope with their unique problems. Principals must take a leadership role in establishing the support groups. They must also be cognizant of the community and government agencies that are available to assist these students and share this information with the families. Special attention should be given to these students until they overcome their problems. Peer counseling is effective. However, peer counselors must be interviewed and trained for this important position. Peer counselors should be caring individuals with good interpersonal skills. Additionally, a teacher or teacher assistant can be paired with these students to provide one-on-one counseling support. Their primary responsibilities would be to meet with the students once a week for about an hour and take the time to listen to what's going on in the students' mind and provide suggestions. Good listening skills are vital to this effort. Many times students have mental anguish because the non-custodial parent appears not to care about their education. If this is the case, school administrators can insist that non-custodial parents attend teacher meetings and school activities. If the custodial and non-custodial parent refuse to meet together, separate sessions can be held.

4. Have High Expectations for Students' Learning

Principals must have high expectations about their students' learning abilities and desires. These high expectations must be instilled in teachers. Principals need to convey that all students can and do want to learn. As stated by the extraordinary Garfield High School math teacher in the motion picture entitled *Stand and Deliver,* "Students will rise to the level of expectation held by teachers." Also while many parents of low SES and African-American students may not have the time, energy, or knowledge to help their children, they strongly want their sons and daughters to learn. While parents may not have the home space and furniture to provide study areas, they will sacrifice to help their offspring gain an education. Setting the proper teacher expectation is crucial because if teachers come to believe incorrectly that these students are unable to learn or are uninterested in learning, teachers will depress their expectations about these students and behave in such a way as to create less learning (Valverde, 1988).

5. Plan in Advance

Family members become frustrated and "turned off" to school involvement when they are provided a short notice to assist with or participate in school functions. This is crisis management and should not occur with proper planning. School administrators must increase the awareness and sensitivity of the school's staff to parents' real time constraints. Insist that the staff announce meetings and other events long enough in advance for parents/family members to arrange for time off from work if necessary. Hold many meetings in the evenings or on the weekends with child care provided. Make daycare/babysitting available for major school activities. Be careful concerning cancelling school at the last minute due to weather conditions, thus leaving many low SES and African-American parents with no resources for the care of their children.

6. Visit the Churches

Go to the churches that many low SES and African-American families attend and request that ministers preach about the importance of parents/family members getting actively involved in the educational activities of the child. Request that the ministers establish tutoring centers at the churches for the children. Get a list of names and phone numbers of potential mentors. Request a list of Sunday School teachers and ask them if they would be interested in serving as tutors in the school. Many churches have programs in place to address the needs of families and children. Find out what the programs are and if the program needs more space, invite them to use the school facilities.

7. Produce Newsletters for Families

Start a "newsletter for families." It is imperative that the newsletters are professionally formatted. Newsletters should be mailed to the homes or to places in the community that families visit frequently. This may be the local grocery store or the recreation center. Request that the community agency display the newsletters in locations highly visible and accessible to families. Topical information for the newsletters should include homework strategies, teacher features, "getting to know you" columns, reports on special projects, and parenting tips. Another option is to get the local newspaper to print the entire student newspaper, plus messages from the principal and staff, in a special page every other Saturday. Newsletters that emerge from the classroom are usually of high interest to parents, especially when their children had a major part in producing them. "Newsletters calendars" that include monthly information of interest to parents and children are valuable. They should include information on forthcoming class activities, special events, parent-teacher meetings, and other important information (Davies, 1991).

8. Try a Parent/Student Switch Day

Institute a "parent/student switch day" program. Excuse the student for a partial day if the parent takes his or her place during that time period. The parent must follow the student's schedule, and be responsible for all work for the partial day. This is a great way to get parents or family members familiar with other school personnel and to give them a profound insight into the inner workings of the school. Many times, the parent's idea of what's going on in the school today is what they experienced while they were in school fifteen years ago. This is not true. Schools have changed quite a bit. Parents/family members will be surprised and elated when they see the computer room and other forms of technology. Also, discuss with politicians and business people the possibility of a tax break for those parents who actively participate in school activities. A deduction, much like the day care deduction, would provide incentive for parents to regularly attend and participate in school activities.

9. Invite Families to Use the School Facilities

Make school libraries open only to children and their families during extended hours. Thus, resources could be available to and accessible to the families and children. Volunteers could perform a range of functions connected with maintaining the library, and family members could share special skills, talents, or interests through a library forum. Open the school facilities for families' use after school hours (i.e., swimming pool and gymnasium for wellness activities, library, theater, meeting room, etc.).

10. Employ Parents as Teacher Aides and Substitute Teachers

Employ parents/family members as teacher aides and substitute teachers within the school. This method would enable the parents/family members to receive training and would assist them in gaining a better understanding of school rules and regulations. In addition, this method would cause some students to cease their negative behavior (Johnson & Johnson, 1990). Students tend not to misbehave when a family member has high visibility in the school.

11. Hold Activities at the Site of Major Employers and get Employers Involved

Many parents live close to their jobs. Usually, the job will have a meeting room. If this is the case, contact the employers and solicit permission to hold programs at the site of the major employers (Stouffer, 1992). Principals, assistant principals, and counselors should periodically schedule lunch sessions with parents at their job sites. Also, principals must be aggressive in contacting businesses and government agencies for assistance in the form of money, tours, tutors, and supplies. Contact hospitals, thrift shops, and farms. Take students on tours to prisons. Many low SES children will know some of the prisoners. This will be a powerful method of reinforcing the need for good behavior. McDonalds Fast Food Restaurant will give tours of the restaurant and provide refreshments free for most children. Ask popular radio stations for weekly radio spots so that an educator or a parent/family member can talk about the activities at school. If this is the case, be sure to give something back to the businesses. For example, the elementary school students can decorate the radio station, serenade the employees, and make valentine cards for them.

12. Get Parents' Input in Disciplinary Measures

Invite a group of parents to visit the school and engage in suggestions for improving discipline problems. This group should meet with a few administrators and teachers in order to become involved in the discussion. There should not be an overpowering number of school staff members present (Johnson & Johnson, 1990). The idea is that parents will become more supportive of disciplinary procedures if they have input into the decision making process. They will also have a better understanding of the school's discipline policy.

13. Initiate a Family Appreciation Night

Organize a special parent and family appreciation night. Ensure that refreshments are served. Introduce or acknowledge some parents by calling their names and asking them to stand. Be sure to include the hard-to-get parents. You may also want to present them a certificate or some other recognition in front of their peers, if they assisted with a previous activity.

14. Ensure that the Initial Thrust is Social

To improve parent/families involvement, especially of those who have seldom if ever been involved, the initial thrust should be social; once they are more involved with the schools, the staff should work toward increased educational involvement (Comer, 1987). Coordinate parent/alumni basketball games using alumni cheerleaders, parents/alumni band concerts, and similar sports and drama events. These are very popular with many low SES and African-American families.

15. Hold Orientations

Provide orientations for parents of students at all grade levels, especially in transition stages (elementary to middle level, from middle level to high school). Include in the orientations administrative presentations, student-guided tour of the facilities, lunch in the cafeteria, visits with counselors and department chairs, and observations of classes during typical school days. Many low income and African-American parents will have no transportation to the orientations. If this is the situation, develop a plan for busing some parents/family members to school activities.

16. Establish a Multicultural Climate

The poor self-image caused by the student's home culture and being ignored or rejected by school personnel produce poor learning and ineffective study habits. These also preclude family involvement. Many families will perceive the school as a place for high income and middle income students. Since principals are the most influential persons in the school, they can assist greatly in creating a compatible cultural climate. First, they must learn about the various cultures by: visiting the homes of low income and African-American students, attending community organized events, joining community organizations, reading the history of the community, learning about the school's history by talking with alumni of the school who are now parents of children attending, reading past newspaper accounts, or taking ethnic studies courses at nearby colleges or universities. Second, principals should find ways to increase their teachers' knowledge and understanding of the various cultures in attendance.

Principals can teach their faculties what they have learned by leading staff development sessions, organizing visits to community events, bringing in members of the community to speak to teachers, setting up a series of lectures by experts representing different cultures, providing reading materials and formalizing reading groups, and encouraging teachers to make home visitations on a regular basis throughout the academic year (Valverde, 1988). There are many multicultural activities that are very effective which principals can share with teachers during staff development sessions. An International Night focusing on food, clothing, and customs is popular. Organizing parent resource teams where parents can share something about their heritage with the children and other parents is a second one.

Involving children and their parents in doing "family trees" and then creating a "hallway of our heritage" (or display the family histories in the community) and bringing parents together to learn about the importance of modeling positive multicultural attitudes are two more. Lastly, educators can make available print and video materials on the lives of people from different cultures, and they can recognize holidays and special events of all of the different cultural and ethnic groups in society in appropriate and positive ways (Swick, 1991).

17. Give a Family Involvement Report Card

The Family Involvement Report Card should have a letter grade. It should grade the family on key involvement activities such as: attendance at meetings, amount of volunteer work in the school, attendance at conferences, and monitoring of homework. Students should sign their parent/family report card. Families should be given a checklist of items which will determine the grade. On the checklist, the criteria for each of the following must be clearly depicted: A, B, C, D, and F. Families who make a grade of "A" should be placed on the honor roll. Families who make a failing grade should be counseled and provided support services.

PRINCIPALS, PARENTS, AND MASLOW

According to Stouffer (1992), family involvement must be a K–12 focus. Between the fifth and eight grades, we "lose" significant numbers of low SES and African-American families who had previously been at least somewhat involved in the academic and curricular lives of their children. Although there are various reasons for this occurrence, a paramount reason is that the families have many needs that are not being satisfied. Principals can effectively address this issue by realizing that parents have diverse needs, many of which can be addressed to some extent through viewing the needs from the perspective of Maslow's Hierarchy of Needs.

Abraham Maslow postulated that human-need structures are organized in a hierarchical system and that needs lower in the hierarchy must be fulfilled before needs higher in the hierarchy become salient. The lowest needs (physiological) are the strongest, and the highest needs (self-actualization) are the weakest. This principle states that the lowest need, having the greatest strength or potency, plays the foremost role in motivating behavior until it is "fairly well" gratified. Then the next need in the hierarchy, having the next-greatest prepotency, becomes the dominant source of motivation, and so on until self-actualization, the highest and weakest need, becomes prepotent.

The ascent of the need hierarchy is thus contingent on the sufficient satisfaction of each prior need. A "chronically gratified" need ceases to be an active organizer of behavior, thereby allowing the next need in the hierarchy to predominate (Arkes & Garske, 1978). Below is a diagram of Maslow's Hierarchy of Needs, followed by specific actions that principals can take at each level to assist in addressing the needs of family members. Principals can plan school activities that will satisfy the needs of family members and simultaneously promote school involvement. For many low SES and African-American families, particular attention should be focused on fulfilling the lower needs.

Maslow's Hierarchy of Needs

Self-Actualization Needs

|

Self-Esteem Needs

|

Social Needs

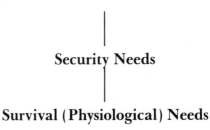

Security Needs

Survival (Physiological) Needs

Self-Actualization Needs

Empower parents. Don't assume that socioeconomically poor parents are poor parents. Work with parents from an empowerment rather than a deficit model of parent involvement.

Give parents/family members opportunities to use their talents in the classroom.

Let them participate in decision making.

Allow them to tutor, counsel, and mentor.

Provide opportunities for self-growth through gaining meaningful experiences.

Self-Esteem Needs

Begin and conclude all parent conferences on positive notes, emphasizing the strengths of the child and parent.

Provide positive news to parents by phone and mail.

Have "Family of the Week" hall displays.

Have a "Grandparents Day."

Praise parents in front of peers at assemblies for a "job well done."

Publicize contributions in the church bulletins and community centers.

Present plaques, trophies, and certificates for contributions immediately at the termination of the activity.

Invite parents to eat breakfast and lunch at the school for no cost.

Publicize parents' contributions in the school newspaper or local city papers (minority parents contributions should also be promulgated in the local minority newspaper).

Announce contributions on the local popular radio station (minority parents' contributions should also be announced over the local minority radio station).

Emphasize positive communications early in the school year.

Hug a parent in public.

Social Needs

Have aerobics classes, dance classes, self-defense classes, bingo, etc., during evenings and weekends at the school.

Provide parenting skills classes during the evenings and weekends on dealing with teenagers, discipline, how to help with homework, or social skills.

Offer parent support groups (single parents, working parents, etc.).

Establish a parent room with coffee and doughnuts available.

Security Needs

Have safety presentations by police officers for parents during evening hours.

Begin a police liaison program offered by the school for student and parent information/assistance.

Offer self-defense classes for parents during the evening hours.

Survival Needs

Start classes in parenting homework/tutoring strategies, drug education, and improving communication skills taught by counselors.

Employ parents as substitute teachers and teachers' aides.

Employ parents as clerical and maintenance workers.

Display job listings for city and state jobs in the parent room.

Assist in locating jobs for students that won't interfere with academics.

Provide a General Educational Development (GED) course at night.

Offer word processing, computer classes, and other skill classes.

PARENT CENTERS

Set aside a room at a centralized location for a parent center. Provide coffee, tea, cookies, and doughnuts. Provide print and video resources on such topics as parenting skills or selection of post-high school career/educational options. The purpose of parent centers is so that parents will feel more positive about the school and more welcome in the school (Stevens, 1992). It should be designed to provide learning experiences for parents to enable them to work more effectively with their children at home. Teachers and students may also take advantage of center activities and resources. A major goal of the parent center would be to bring parent/family members together by providing a variety of material, equipment, and information useful in working with their children. The Center should offer some morning, afternoon, and evening hours to accommodate working and non-working parents. The following should be in the Center:

Information and publications on ways to help children.

A library of books, toys, educational games, equipment, and computers that parents can check out and take home.

Parent newsletters

Job listings

A take-home computer program for parents to use with their children.

All items that a parent/family member check out and take home should be for the purpose of increasing the academic skills of the students, and supporting homework efforts. To be effective, a check out or lending policy should be implemented. If this is not the case, much friction will develop between educators and parents concerning accountability. Below is an accountability model that you can use:

Parent Center Accountability Form

Dear Parent/Family Member,

We are pleased that you want to check out materials from your parent/family center, but before you take the materials home, please sign the agreement below, assuring us that you are aware of your responsibilities.

Thank you for your cooperation.

Sincerely,

Principal

I, the undersigned parent/family member, understand that I am responsible for the borrowed materials in the following ways:

1. I will see that the materials are properly used in my home.

2. I will supervise my children while they use the borrowed materials.

3. I will return materials on or before the due date.

Parent/Family Member Signature   *Date*

* Parent/Family Member may checkout the items for no more than one week at a time.

In the parent center there should be a computer lab with several computers. The computer instruction should have highly user-friendly, individualized, and self-paced programs. It should offer a variety of learning experiences for parents and students. Teachers should obligate time to the lab during the mornings or evenings to teach computer literacy to provide the parents/family members with enough knowledge to handle operation of the computers on their own. Software should be available to include typing tutors, word processing, computer graphics, and database programs. The computer lab should be a place for parents/family members to improve their reading and math skills and to work on life study skills. Life study skills would include topics such as filing income taxes, time management, and job success. These are very popular with parents and there is a tremendous amount of excellent software available. Parents should also be encouraged to bring their children to the lab for reading and math skills practice. The lab should have several software program games that are just for fun.

Another purpose of the parent center is for administrators and teachers. It is a valuable and time saving resource. Parents are readily available to contact other parents to relay information about problems at school, medicine that may be urgently needed, and arrangements for school social functions. Parents will also be available to order teaching materials or offer comfort to children in a moment of crisis. Parents would be highly visible in the school. A parent center can be organized in any school. The cost is low; money from Chapter I and other special programs can be used, or small grants from local businesses or foundations may be obtained. Several considerations are vital when setting up a Center.

1. One or two paid parents of students in the school should coordinate the Parent Center and aggressively recruit more parent volunteers. The parents should be paid about three dollars above the minimum wage.

2. Obtain a classroom with a sofa, table, file cabinet, phone, bulletin board, coffee pot, microwave oven, and snack machines. The Center should also sponsor English-as-a-second-language (ESL) and General Education Development (GED) classes for parents.

HOME VISITING AND HOME VISITOR PROGRAMS

Principals can establish an environment to promote home visiting by teachers and counselors, or they can institute a Home Visitor Program employing parents or family members on a paid basis. Home visiting is an effective means of providing parents and teachers a time for exploring their common concerns, sharing information on child development and learning, and laying a foundation for having a positive relationship (Young Children, 1990). The opportunity for close contact between teacher and parent is invaluable for building trust and empathy. Home visits are usually scheduled on a weekly or monthly basis with each visit lasting about one hour. It is essential that all home visitors undergo a training program. Parents should be notified well in advance before each visit through telephone calls, letters mailed to the home address, or memos given to the students to deliver to the parents. Home visits are especially effective for parents of kindergarten, early elementary school students, and students with special needs. Teachers can share instructional activities with the parents and explain to the parents how to assist their children with the activities. Home visiting more effectively extends the school in the home and assists parents in becoming effective teachers of their children.

Home visitors cannot be shy and some teachers may need to go with more experienced teachers in this area until they feel comfortable. Tolerance and flexibility are important in that teachers will see many things they do not normally see in their own environment. They may have to sit on the end of the bed while talking to a parent or talk with a parent in the apartment's laundromat. However, the rewards from successful home visits are significant. Parents will come to school and ask to see these teachers frequently. Parents' and children's attitudes about homework and school will become more positive. Important activities to conduct during home visits include demonstrating home learning packets, interpreting learning styles inventories, explaining progress reports and report cards, and sharing available school and community resources. Teachers should have available phone numbers and contact persons for agencies such as mental health agencies and the Department of Children Services to share with the families.

Patience and persistency are required in all home visits. When teachers request that students show them where the students' live, students have been known to lead teachers to several incorrect addresses before directing the teachers to the correct house or apartment. These students perceive this situation as being a game. They are endeavoring to test the patience of the teachers. They think the teachers will become frustrated and cease trying to locate the correct house. In some home visits, parents will not want to invite teachers into their house or will not come outside of the house to converse with the teachers. Do not let this upset you. Many teachers inform me that an effective technique in this type of situation with a difficult parent is to bring a small gift or take some food. If this is ineffective, phone them on the job or phone another significant family member such as the grandmother and communicate your concerns about the child. Again, the idea is to let the parents know that you will not give up your attempts at making contact.

The purpose of the Parent Home Visitor Program is to have parents or family members who are recruited, interviewed, and paid to go into the housing projects or low income neighborhoods to recruit other family members into the school or to disseminate information and materials to these family members about school activities. These coordinators will be a liaison between the teachers, counselors, social workers and the families living in low income neighborhoods.

The coordinators should be parents/family members who are actively involved in the community, such as: deacons in churches, officers in local civic groups, leaders in churches, or leaders of community organizations. They should be well respected and should have lived in the community for a substantial number of years. Their personality can be fairly aggressive, however, it is imperative that they possess excellent interpersonal and communication skills. The coordinators will disseminate information to families about school expectations, the curriculum, rules, and requirements. They will dispense advice and materials on how the family members can better help children with their work in school. They will encourage parents of elementary students to read regularly to their children at home.

SUMMARY

Demographic projections indicate that poor, urban, and minority students will increasingly dominate public schools in the next decade and well into the 21st century. For example, the student bodies of school districts in Atlanta, Newark, Washington, D.C., and San Antonio are over 90 percent "minority" (Condition of Education, 1986). While the minority student population of U.S. schools has been continuously increasing into the majority category, the educational achievement of minority students across the country has remained below that of their White counterparts. Many of these students are from low SES families, African-American families, and Hispanic families. This "new" majority demands that public schools seriously reassess and revise their policies, programs, and procedures to respond more effectively to their unique needs, to improve the quality of this student population's school experiences, and to enhance its academic achievement (Gay, 1988). Critical to accomplishing this is obtaining the involvement of the families in the education of their children. Principals are the most effective change agents in accomplishing this.

It is well documented in effective schools research (Edmonds & Frederiksen, 1978) that principals set the tone of the schools, and if they stay long enough at a school, they put their "fingerprints" on the school. My suggestions in this chapter will allow principals to put effective "fingerprints" on the school. The theme of this chapter is to be proactive and innovative in encouraging parent/family involvement. School administrators must believe that all parents care about their children. Principals must convey to teachers that all parents have the abilities, when properly supported, to help their child succeed in school.

ACTIVITIES FOR THE READERS

1. What behaviors can principals model to instill in teachers high expectations for academic achievement and good behavior from all students? What behaviors can teachers model in the classroom to convey to all students that they are expected to achieve and behave in class? What behaviors can teachers model in conferences with parents/family members that will convey to them that the teachers have high expectations for their children? Should expectations be both high and realistic? Justify your answer.

2. Visit at least five schools with "newsletters for families." Prepare a report to the class on your impression of the newsletter and your perceptions of its effectiveness. Include in your report the extent of the involvement of the students in writing and printing the newsletter and how frequently the newsletters are published.

3. Interview principals or assistant principals at five schools. Find out the number of low SES and African-American parents/family mem-

bers of students in the school that are employed as teacher aides and substitute teachers. Ascertain from the assistant principal and the appropriate classroom teachers if the high visibility of the parents/family members in these positions have a positive impact on the behaviors and academics of their students.

3. Phone some major employers of a significant number of low income and minority families of students from a nearby school. Find out if they would be receptive to the school, using their facilities to hold school activities and meetings. Is there a fee involved? Have they received any prior requests from schools for assistance in this area?

4. Discuss the purpose of Maslow's Hierarchy of Needs. Why is it called a hierarchical system? Why is it valuable to school administrators as a tool to facilitate parent/family involvement? How can a principal use it to facilitate parent/family involvement in the school? How can classroom teachers use it to facilitate parent/family involvement in the classroom?

5. What are some major components that should be planned to institute an effective Home Visitor Program? What are major considerations in hiring parents to coordinate this program? Do you feel this is a cost effective method of enhancing parent/family involvement? Justify your answer.

6. Interview several parent involvement coordinators from Chapter I programs. Find out the strategies they use that work best in facilitating parental involvement. How do they define parental involvement? Describe the workshops they give to parents and teachers on parent involvement or parent education strategies. Tour the facilities and resources they have and list with a brief description all the major resources including books, videos, computer programs, films, etc. Discuss your opinions of the adequacy of resources and effectiveness in carrying out their mission.

Chapter Five

ADDITIONAL TOPICS OF CONCERN

INCIDENTAL LEARNING THROUGH ROLE MODELS

Many positive behaviors and positive values that educators impart to the students at school are not reinforced by the families in the home. In fact, in many instances there are forces at home that destroy the positive values taught by educators and ingrain in the students negative attributes that are not conducive to good academic motivation and achievement. A powerful force that educators need to address through conferences, written communications, and phone communications with family members is transferring negative behaviors and negative values to children through incidental learning.

Low SES and many African-American students learn much from family members through incidental learning that is carried into the classroom. As children observe these influential family members or role models on a consistent basis, the models engender incidental learning (Good & Brophy, 1991). Incidental learning is a social learning term denoting that children learn by watching an influential adult role model's behavior and the consequences of the behavior. The model may be verbalizing one message but his or her behavior may be sending a different and a more negative message to the children. In this case, the children will learn what is contrary to the model's intentions. If there is a discrepancy between parents' preaching and parents' practice, children will tend to do as the parents do, not as they say. Numerous significant family members teach children this hidden agenda which is inconsistent with and detracts from the teachings of the school relative to proper behavior and academic achievement.

Family members may not be conscious that they are transmitting these behaviors. Children pick up cues that inform them how to react in pressure and angry situations, how to treat other adults and peers, and how high a value should be placed on education. Many experimental studies confirm the powerful effects of incidental learning (Welch &

Tisdale, 1986). The studies show that a child copies behaviors more completely when the model is perceived to be powerful, in control, and similar to the child. Children can be taught positive behaviors such as goal-oriented thinking and problem solving skills by parents through incidental learning. Many students, especially those from low SES and minority backgrounds, fail to develop an adequate appreciation of their own potential for affecting the world through goal-oriented thinking and problem solving (Bandura, 1989). They tend to feel helpless in the face of frustration or adversity, and have learned to think in terms of passively accepting their fate rather than actively shaping it. Teachers can facilitate these families use of incidental learning as a powerful teaching tool to reinforce classroom values by following my suggestions below. These suggestions may be promulgated to families through conferences, newsletters, notes given to children to take home, and phone communications.

1. Modeling Problem Solving Skills

According to research, many low achieving students traditionally aren't taught critical thinking skills such as problem solving. With these students, teachers traditionally focused on teaching the basic skills. However, to increase motivation and achievement an equal focus should be placed on teaching basic skills and critical thinking skills. In addition to the teacher focusing on these skills in the classroom, they can teach parents how to convey problem solving skills to their children through modeling and incidental learning. This can be accomplished by telling family members that when they are helping children with their homework not to simply give the children the correct answer but to tell them why the answer is correct and the thinking processes that were employed to arrive at the correct answer. Inform parents that whenever any problem at home has to be solved such as repairing the lawn mower, repairing the plumbing, or repairing the car, the parent should think out loud while solving the problem so that children can model the thought processes involved.

2. Modeling Placing a High Importance on Learning

Family members should be informed that whenever a child asks an academic question and the family member is not prepared to answer, all possible attempts should be made to seek an answer to the question. The family member should promise the child that he/she will get the answer or ask the child to go to the library or some other pertinent resource to seek the answer. This behavior lets the child know that learning is important and worth pursuing. Too many times low SES parents/family members tell the child that they don't know the answer to an academic question and then go about the routine of life. This behavior imparts to the child that the pursuit of knowledge is not important and there are many more important things in life than school.

Secondly, when a child goes to the library to work on an assignment, the child should not go alone. Some significant family member should accompany the child. The family member should remain in the library until the child has completed the assignment. Asking the child how long it will take to complete the assignment, and telling the child that you will leave the library and return when he has finished it transmit a clear negative message. The message is that the student should hurry up and complete the assignment and the assignment has little worth. It is a good idea for the family member to stay the entire time with the child in the library and to assist the child. The family member should read a book, newspaper item of interest, or magazine while waiting. When the child has finished the library assignment, check out your book, show it to the child, and explain your interest in the book. Modeling of the aforementioned positive behaviors will result in the child realizing that academics are important because significant adults in his or her learning environment behave as though it is important. When the teacher helps the family member in developing these behaviors, the student will demonstrate augmented motivation and achievement in the classroom.

3. Modeling Good Social Skills (Rules and Procedures)

Many teachers will say repeatedly that children in the classroom bring poor social skills from home that hinder teaching and learning. The subpar social skills result in a disregard for classroom rules and procedures, and lead to classroom disruptions such as fighting, talking back to teachers, and putting other students down who are endeavoring to take part in class discussions. This negative energy detracts significantly from time on task and leaves the teacher with much mental frustration and exhaustion at the end of the school day. Many low SES parents do not adequately teach their kids how to cope with the world and its problems in a rational manner. They become quick to strike out and fight when teased by other students because they don't know the rational alternatives.

Family members should be informed through diverse means that their children should not simply be cited rigid rules and consequences. They must also model and spell out the underlying reasons for rules and decisions. Children will be more receptive to accepting and internalizing rules that they can understand. Parents/family members cannot assume that children are capable of figuring out the rules by themselves, regardless of their grade level. When rules are not explained, children will see adults as flaunting power or acting arbitrarily. With a proper explanation that is connected to moral development, they will see rules and decisions in the home as thoughtful endeavors to shape values and attitudes that result in good social skills.

Lastly, all significant family members must be informed that there must be rules in the house for all persons. The rules must be clearly promulgated. Children must see adults complying with the rules. Adults must be quick to convey to students that all persons in society have rules and procedures that they must follow. Following the rules and procedures will make them better citizens. By providing guidance to families on the aforementioned points, there will be a significant carryover to the classroom. Students will be more receptive to understanding and complying with classroom rules and procedures. Discipline problems will decrease and time on task and achievement will increase.

4. Modeling Good Social Skills (Respect for Others)

Families can help children learn politeness and good manners by modeling the behaviors they preach. When children show politeness and good manners, they also show concern for the feelings of others and respect for their dignity. Parents can function as positive role models for these behaviors by treating their children and their children's friends in a respectful manner and tone of voice. Do not incessantly nag and criticize. Particularly, do not criticize children in front of their peers.

Positive role modeling should be displayed in all interactions with adults whenever the children are observing. The words **please** and **thank you** must be used frequently. Speak to the adults in a respectful tone of voice. Practice the Golden Rule, "Do unto others as you would have them do unto you." If teachers teach parents/family members the above information, then their children will be more inclined to respect other students in the classroom. My research and experiences show that numerous families are lacking in this area because the pressures of a complex society and the difficult struggle for survival have steered them away from the Golden Rule. In fact, many of the low SES parents of kids in the public schools have never had the Golden Rule ingrained in them during their formative adolescent years.

5. Modeling Good Listening Skills

Families must be informed of the value of being a good listener to their children. This is a vital parenting skill but one which is lacking in many families in the 90's. This behavior can be successfully modeled by family members, making the time to listen to their children. When children are talking, hear them out. Do not cut them off or say that you have other chores to do. The above politeness should be demonstrated in conversations with adults. By doing this, children will acquire good listening habits and transfer them into the classroom. This would be beneficial during small group work because students will not interrupt other students that are talking. Students will also be less inclined to display off task behaviors while the teacher is lecturing or explaining directions.

ASIAN-AMERICANS' PARENTAL EXPECTATIONS

Many effective strategies can be learned from the success of Asian-American high school students that would benefit low SES and African-American families. Asian-Americans comprise approximately two percent of the national population, but they earn 2.6 percent of all bachelor degrees and 3.4 percent of all doctoral degrees awarded each year. Asian-American students earn one-fifth of the Ph.D's in physical sciences, 18 percent of the doctoral degrees in engineering, and about one-quarter of all the doctorates awarded in the life sciences (Hsia, 1988). The phenomenal success of Asian-Americans has led to stereotypes regarding their academic prowess. For example, when 25 elementary school teachers were given personal data cards on fictitious students, they assigned the Asian-American students higher grades and expected them to attain higher occupational status than the other students (Tom, 1983). When one segment of the nation outshines all others there has to be a logical reason.

(Reglin & Adams, 1990) conducted a descriptive research study to investigate this phenomenon. The researchers surveyed 129 high school students using a "Cultural Comparison Questionnaire." The theoretical framework for the study revolved around the helplessness hypothesis and the home influence hypothesis. The helplessness hypothesis states that learned helplessness is a psychological state in which repeated failure to control the outcome of ones' situation induces a carryover of passivity and a depressed level of performance to a new situation. The home influence hypothesis suggests that children of parents with low expectations do better than children of parents with high expectations. This study has much significance for educators who work with significant numbers of low SES and African-American students because both hypotheses are applicable to these students. The specific research question addressed in this study was: Do cultural differences between families of Asian-American high school students and non-Asian high school students contribute to the Asian-Americans' greater success in high school?

Two major findings from this study have important implications for educators and parents/family members of unmotivated and underachieving children. Firstly, no Asian-American wanted to be a professional athlete, while a significant number of non-Asians wanted to be professional athletes. More than a third of the Asian-Americans wanted to be famous scientists, while only 4.3 percent of the non-Asians wanted to be famous scientists. Secondly, a greater number of the non-Asian students watched more TV each week.

Many low SES and African-American students devote a tremendous number of hours in playing sports such as basketball and watching athletic events on television. (Morris, 1990) contended that the media's penchant for glamorizing Black male athletes and entertainers as opposed to academically successful Black male role models may lead to the unrealistic view that nonacademic pursuits are higher probability roads to success. Educators must convey to parents/family members that students' chances of becoming a Michael Jordan or Larry Byrd are very slim. Parents/family members, especially males, reinforce the children's aspirations to become super athletes. This is accomplished by incessantly praising the professional athletes and giving little praise and attention to other vital professionals such as: lawyers, teachers, doctors, barbers, engineers, scientists, and bank managers. Educators must make families conscious that they are providing unrealistic expectations for the children. The many hours on the basketball courts deprive the children of numerous opportunities to gain valuable educational experiences. Through conferences and parent education workshops, educators must change this behavior in parents and teach them to model behaviors that will greatly reinforce academic goals. Parents/family members can do this in a variety of ways such as: frequently discussing role models like Governor Wilder of Virginia and General Colin Powell, watching fewer athletic events on TV, watching more educational events, encouraging the children to read articles in the newspaper besides the sports section, and taking the children on trips to nearby cultural sites. Low SES and African-American families must be guided into making sports and entertainment a lesser part of their culture and academic achievement a greater part of the culture.

Parental control of, interest in, and expectations for their children work hand in hand to help mold successful and learned students. It is imperative that parents and teachers positively impact the television viewing habits of the children to engender learned students. Television's socializing effects are greater for low SES and African-American children because of the phenomenal amount of time they spend watching television. Many times these children weekly television watching exceeds their parents 40-hour work week. These families are often less mobile and less able to afford alternative forms of entertainment and baby sitters. Low SES and African-American children are more susceptible to television effects because they often use television as a source of guidance. For example, these adolescents have reported using television to learn dating behavior and about different occupations.

Television can negatively affect the students' self-concept. Aggressive behavior on television is more likely to be imitated by children when aggression is part of their real-life experience. Thus, low SES and African-American children, many of whom live in violence-prone neighborhoods in large cities, are especially at risk of imitating violent behavior. Television provides these adolescents an outlet for utilizing time that could be better spent developing intellectual, artistic, interpersonal, mechanical, and manual skills. Heavy television viewing has been associated with lower imagination and less creativity. Below are some suggestions for parents/family members and educators that can eliminate many of the negative effects of television.

1) Parents/family members should control the amount of time children spend passively with the media and encourage them to engage in more activities conducive to intellectual and physical growth (trips to the zoo and museum, and watching public educational television shows).

2) Parents/family members need to watch television with children and point out the applicability of what is shown on television to children's everyday interactions.

3) Parents/family members need to monitor what children watch and

encourage viewing of shows such as: Cosby Show, 20/20, 60 Minutes, and Family Matters.

4) Parents/family members should work on behalf of the child outside of home to pressure society to change by working with interested citizens for better media in their community.

5) Teachers should develop assignments and learning activities that revolve around assigned television shows such as writing a comparative analysis of how "ROOTS" is treated on the television show and in the book.

6) Teachers need to become familiar with and augment curricula designed to teach children to evaluate television content.

7) School Administrators need to introduce training for critical viewing into their local school system.

SUMMARY

Achievement test scores will remain low for a substantial number of low SES and minority students until educators place a greater focus on educating parents. Behaviors exhibited by parents/families at home can reinforce or subtract from the academic efforts in the school. Families are important role models. By making them cognizant of the powerful effects of incidental learning and modeling, families can become positive role models. This requires an innovative way of looking at teaching and learning. Families must be trained to be teachers and good role models. Negative forces in the home can unlearn many of the positive behaviors taught to students in the classroom. Educators must change some of the cultural habits of low SES and African-American students. Educators must encourage parents to model behaviors that will demonstrate to children that role models such as doctors, engineers, and lawyers are more important than athletes and entertainers. The work ethic and high parental expectations for academics are profoundly ingrained in the culture of Asian-American students. Both must become a significant factor in the culture of all students.

ACTIVITIES FOR THE READERS

1. What is meant by incidental learning? How would you introduce this concept to parents during a parent-teacher conference? Why is it relatively useless for parents/family members to tell students to "Do as I

say, not as I do?" What behaviors should a new teacher model during the first meeting with a parent to convey to the parent a profound interest in working with him/her as a partner?

2. Many teachers are complaining that numerous low SES students are coming to school with poor social skills which make teaching and learning difficult. Interview an elementary teacher, a middle school teacher, and a high school teacher. Ask them to define social skills. Ask them about the appropriateness of the social skills of the students in their classroom. Interview three parents of low SES children and ask them to define social skills. Compare and contrast the definitions. Are any definitions similar to your definition of social skills? What can you do as a classroom teacher to make parents/family members more sensitive to modeling proper social skills? What can you do in the classroom to reinforce proper social skills? How much time will this require from you?

3. How does television rob many low SES and African-American students of opportunities for good educational experiences? What advice would you give to parents/family members that could assist them in rectifying this situation? What are some class activities that would be effective in teaching students good television viewing habits? List several ways you would employ the television as an effective teaching aid.

CONCLUSION

Some critics of involving low SES and minority families in school programs feel that many efforts to involve parents in the programs represent nothing more than an attempt to involve these parents simply for the sake of involving them. These critics feel that family involvement response is one which is being undertaken by educators simply because it is fashionable and legislatively necessary to do so without any real belief or commitment on their part to the process. As stated throughout this text, research clearly shows that family involvement is crucial to the academic motivation and achievement of all children. Educators must view the families as wanting to get involved but needing a stimulus in the form of one of the innovative strategies delineated in this text to make this happen.

Family members must be seen as educators because **real** learning is not confined to the school. While it is true that some of these parents/family members don't know how to educate their children, this is surely not true of all of them. However, those who don't know how to educate their children can learn how to do so. Two key ingredients that educators must have to effectively assist parents/family members to educate their children are creativity and patience. Educators can employ creativity to identify the talents of the parents, extend an invitation to come to the school and use their talents, establish support programs during the evening hours or on the weekend to address the families immediate concerns, and be sensitive to practicing good human relations skills at all times. Patience is needed in that there are usually myriad and diverse reasons that occurred over a long period of time which precluded school involvement and led to a misperception that family members do not care about the academics of the children. These barriers are not easy to tear down and they may still be present to some degree after attempting an innovative strategy. Educators must work to get parents/families involved as early as feasible in the school life of the students. They must be patient and persistent in their efforts. Educators must be bold and willing to try different strategies.

It is imperative that schools have many and different school involvement activities for families that lead toward positive high visibility. Participating in volunteer training programs, helping recruit other volunteers, making instructional materials at home, sharing their talents with the school, helping plan social functions, assisting with field trips, assisting with individual class projects, and observing the classroom are good positive traditional high visibility goals (Firth, 1985). However, there are additional innovative high visibility options that are effective with many of these parents. Encourage the parents/family members to donate plants, paint, tables, and similar items that would make the classroom, teachers' lounge, or library more attractive and useful.

A second technique is to encourage the parents/family members to surprise the teachers with a baked cake or cookies, fresh fruit, vegetables, or a small gift from the store as a gesture of appreciation. Ask them to attach a card signed by several family members and the student. The student should present it to the teacher. Thirdly, ask the parents/family members to mail inexpensive "thank you" cards expressing interest and appreciation to all of the significant persons at the school that positively impacted the academic success of the child. This should include administrators, teachers, coaches, the lunchroom manager, the secretary, librarians, counselors, and custodians. These people will spread "good will" about the parents/family members throughout the school and their names will be held in high esteem. There are many innovative school involvement strategies other than those listed throughout the text that will work with low SES and African-American parents/family members. The number of strategies available are only limited by the imagination, determination, and energy of the educator.

BIBLIOGRAPHY

Arkes, H.R., & Garske, J.P. (1978). *Psychological theories of motivation.* Monterey, CA: Brookes/Cole.

Ascher, C. (1988). Improving the school-home connection for poor and minority urban students. *The Urban Review, 20*(2), 109–123.

Austin, J. (1991). Involving noncustodial parents in their student's education. *NASSP Bulletin, 76*(543), 49–53.

Bandura, A. (1989). Human agency in social cognitive theory. *American Psychologist, 44*(9), 1175–1184.

Barney, J.T., & Koford, L. (1987). Families as partners in the decision-making process. *NASSP Bulletin, 76*(543), 15–23.

Bradley, B. (1988, October). First high school graduates of the 21st century. *Children and Teens Today, 3*(2), 17–19.

Brandt, R.S. (1986). On improving achievement of minority children: A conversation with James Comer. *Educational Leadership, 43*(5), 13–17.

Burchard, J., & Burchard, S. (1987). *Prevention of delinquent behavior.* Newbury Park, CA: Sage.

Burland, J. (1984). "Dysfunctional parenthood in a deprived population." In *Parenthood: A psychodynamic perspective,* edited by R. Cohen, B. Cohler, and S. Weissman. Guilford.

Carlson, C.I. (1990). "Best practices in working with single-parent and stepparent family systems." In *Best practices in school psychology-II,* edited by A. Thomas and J. Grimes, Washington, D.C.: National Association of School Psychologists.

Clark, R.M. (1989). *Home learning activities and children's literacy achievement.* Unpublished Manuscript.

Clay, P.L. (1980). *School policy in observing rights of noncustodial parents.* Network, Columbia, NY: National Committee for Citizens in Education.

Comer, J. (1987). New Haven's school-community connection. *Educational Leadership, 44*(6), 13–16.

Office of Educational Research and Improvement. (1986). *The condition of education.* Washington, DC: U.S. Government Printing Office.

Consortium for Longitudinal Studies. (1981). *Lasting effects in early education.* Monographs of the Society for Research in Child Development.

Davies, D. (1987). Looking for an ecological solution. *Equity and Choice, 4*(1), 3–7.

Davies, D. (1991). Schools reaching out: Family, school and community partnerships for student success. *Phi Delta Kappan, 72*(5), 376–382.

Duncan, C.P. (1992). Parental support in schools and the changing family structure. *NASSP Bulletin, 76*(543), 10–14.

Edelman, M. (1987). *Families in peril: An agenda for social change.* Cambridge: Harvard.

Edler, D. (1981). Ability-grouping as a self-fulfilling prophecy: A meta-analysis of teacher-student interaction. *Sociology of Education, 54*(3), 151–162.

Edmonds, R., & Frederiksen, J. (1985). *Search for effective schools: The identification and the analysis of city schools that are instructionally effective for poor children.* Cambridge: Harvard University, Center for Urban Studies.

Edwards, P.A., & Young, L.S. (1992). Beyond partners: Family, community, and school involvement. *Phi Delta Kappan, 74*(1), 72–81.

Frith, T. (1985). *Secrets parents should know about public schools.* New York: Simon and Schuster.

Garbarino, J. (1982). *Children and families in the social environment.* New York: Aldine.

Gay, G. (1988). Designing relevant curricula for diverse learners. *Education and Urban Society, 20*(4), 327–340.

Good, T.L., & Brophy, J.E. (1991). *Looking in classrooms.* New York: HarperCollins.

Greene, A.L., & Vandegrift, J.A. (1992). Rethinking parent involvement. *Educational Leadership, 50*(1), 57–59.

Hess, R.D. (1980). "Experts and amateurs: Some unintended consequences of parent education." In *Parenting in a Multicultural Society,* eds. M. Fantini and R. Cardenas. New York: Longman.

Hsia, J. (1988). Asian-Americans fight the myth of the super student. *Educational Record, 68,*(4), 94–97.

Hyde, D. (1991). School-parent collaboration results in academic achievement. *NASSP Bulletin, 76*(543), 39–42.

Jackson, B.L., Davies, D., Cooper, B.S., & Page, P. (1988). *Parents make a difference: An evaluation of the New York city public schools' 1987-1988 parent involvement program.* Boston: Institute for Responsive Education and Fordham University.

Johnson, S.O., & Johnson, V.J. (1990). *Better discipline: A practical approach.* Springfield, IL: Charles C Thomas, Publisher.

Jennings, J.M. (1992). Parent involvement strategies for inner-city schools. *NASSP Bulletin, 76*(548), 63–68.

Landfried, S.E. (1991). Educational enabling: When protecting children fosters dependence. *PTA Today, 16*(7), 18–20.

Lewis, D. (1992). *The forgotten factor in school success: The family.* Washington, DC: Home and School Institute.

Mcloughlin, C.S. (1987). *Parent-teacher conferencing.* Springfield, IL: Charles C Thomas, Publisher.

Morris, R. (1992). *Solving the problems of youth at-risk: Involving parents and community resources.* Lancaster, PA: Technomic, pp. 138–144.

Newmann, F. (1981). Reducing student alienation in high schools: Implications of theory. *Harvard Education Review, 51*(4), 546–564.

Nichols, M. (1990). *The nurturing center.* Columbia, SC: Mimeo.

Prosise, R.D. (1990). The home/school relationship from an administrative perspective. *Illinois School Journal, 69*(2), 41–48.

Reglin, G.L. (1990). A model program for educating at-risk students. *Technological Horizons in Education Journal, 17*(6), 65–67.

Reglin, G.L., & Adams, D.R. (1990). Why Asian-American high school students have higher grade point averages and SAT scores than other high school students. *High School Journal, 73*(3), 143–149.

Reglin, G.L. (1993). *Motivating low achieving students: A special focus on unmotivated and underachieving African-American Students.* Springfield, IL: Charles C Thomas, Publisher.

Reglin, G.L., & Amen, J. (1992). Stress and the high school senior: Implications for instruction. *NASSP Bulletin, 76*(548), 78–84.

Sandfort, J.A. (1987). Putting parents in their place in the public schools. *NASSP Bulletin, 71*(496), 99–103.

Smith, T. (1980). *Parents and preschool.* Oxford Preschool Research Project (vol. 6). Ypsilanti, MI: High/Scope.

Sowell, T. (1992, December 3). Young blacks fall victim to racial hype. *The Charlotte Observer,* pp. 4C.

Stevens, L.J. (1992). Meeting the challenge of educating children at risk. *Phi Delta Kappan,* 18–23.

Stouffer, B. (1992, April). We can increase parent involvement in secondary schools. *NASSP Bulletin, 76*(543), 1–9.

Swap, S. (1990). *Parent involvement and success for all children: What we know.* Boston, MA: Institute for Responsive Education.

Sweet, J.A., & Bumpass, L.L. (1988). *American families and households.* New York: Russell Sage Foundation.

Swick, K.J. (1991). *Teacher-parent partnerships to enhance school success in early childhood education.* Washington, DC: National Education Association.

Togerson, G.L. (1990). Toward a critical constructivist approach to school administration: Invisibility, legitimation, and the study of non-events. *Educational Administration Quarterly, 26*(1), 5–37.

Tom, D.Y.H. (1983). *Teacher cognitive style, expectations, and attributions for student performance.* Paper Presented at the Annual Convention of the American Psychological Association.

Tom, D.Y.H., & Cooper, H. (1984). *Academic attributes for success and failure among Asian-Americans.* Paper presented at the Annual Meeting of the American Educational Research Association.

Valverde, L.A. (1988). Principals creating better schools in minority communities. *Education and the Urban Society, 20*(4), 319–327.

Wanat, C. (1991). Meeting the needs of single-parent children: School and parent views differ. *NASSP Bulletin, 76*(543), 43–48.

Welch, F.C., & Tisdale, P.C. (1986). *Between teacher and parent.* Springfield, IL: Charles C Thomas, Publisher.

Young Children. (1990). Raising children in the 1990's: The challenges for parents, educators, and business. *Young Children, 45*(2), 2–3.

INDEX